Singapore MATH

LEVEL 1 A&B

Thinking Kids®
An imprint of Carson-Dellosa Publishing LLC
Greensboro, North Carolina

Copyright © 2015 Singapore Asia Publishers Pte. Ltd.

Thinking Kids®
An imprint of Carson-Dellosa Publishing LLC
PO Box 35665
Greensboro, NC 27425 USA

Printed in the USA • All rights reserved.   ISBN 978-1-4838-1318-9
10-272207784

Table of Contents

Introduction to Singapore Math...5

1A Learning Outcomes 15

Formula Sheet 16

Unit 1:   Numbers 1–10 19

Unit 2:   Fun with Number Bonds 30

Review 1 37

Unit 3:   Adding Numbers up to 10 41

Unit 4:   Subtracting Numbers up to 10 51

Review 2 62

Unit 5:   Shapes and Patterns 68

Unit 6:   Ordinal Numbers 74

Review 3 81

Unit 7:   Numbers 1–20 85

Unit 8:   Adding and Subtracting Numbers up to 20 93

Unit 9:   Length 102

Review 4 108

Mid-Review...112

Challenge Questions 119

Singapore Math Level 1A & 1B

Table of Contents

1B Learning Outcomes...123

Formula Sheet 124

Unit 10:   Mass 127

Unit 11:   Picture Graphs 134

Review 5 141

Unit 12:   Numbers 1–40 146

Unit 13:   Mental Calculations 159

Unit 14:   Multiplying 161

Review 6 169

Unit 15:   Dividing..174

Unit 16:   Time...178

Review 7 182

Unit 17:   Numbers 1–100 187

Unit 18:   Money (Part 1) 201

Unit 19:   Money (Part 2) 206

Review 8 212

Final Review 217

Challenge Questions 224

Solutions 227

Notes 251

INTRODUCTION TO SINGAPORE MATH

Welcome to Singapore Math! The math curriculum in Singapore has been recognized worldwide for its excellence in producing students highly skilled in mathematics. Students in Singapore have ranked at the top in the world in mathematics on the *Trends in International Mathematics and Science Study* (TIMSS) in 1993, 1995, 2003, and 2008. Because of this, Singapore Math has gained in interest and popularity in the United States.

Singapore Math curriculum aims to help students develop the necessary math concepts and process skills for everyday life and to provide students with the ability to formulate, apply, and solve problems. Mathematics in the Singapore Primary (Elementary) Curriculum cover fewer topics but in greater depth. Key math concepts are introduced and built on to reinforce various mathematical ideas and thinking. Students in Singapore are typically one grade level ahead of students in the United States.

The following pages provide examples of the various math problem types and skill sets taught in Singapore.

At an elementary level, some simple mathematical skills can help students understand mathematical principles. These skills are the counting-on, counting-back, and crossing-out methods. Note that these methods are most useful when the numbers are small.

1. The Counting-On Method

Used for addition of two numbers. Count on in 1s with the help of a picture or number line.

$$7 + 4 = \mathbf{11}$$

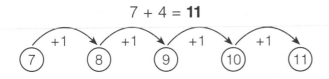

2. The Counting-Back Method

Used for subtraction of two numbers. Count back in 1s with the help of a picture or number line.

$$16 - 3 = \mathbf{13}$$

3. The Crossing-Out Method

Used for subtraction of two numbers. Cross out the number of items to be taken away. Count the remaining ones to find the answer.

$$20 - 12 = \mathbf{8}$$

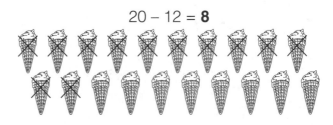

A **number bond** shows the relationship in a simple addition or subtraction problem. The number bond is based on the concept "part-part-whole." This concept is useful in teaching simple addition and subtraction to young children.

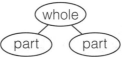

To find a whole, students must add the two parts.
To find a part, students must subtract the other part from the whole.

The different types of number bonds are illustrated on the next page.

5

1. Number Bond (single digits)

3 (part) + 6 (part) = **9** (whole)

9 (whole) − 3 (part) = **6** (part)

9 (whole) − 6 (part) = **3** (part)

2. Addition Number Bond (single digits)

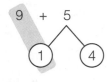

= 9 + 1 + 4   Make a ten first.

= 10 + 4

= **14**

3. Addition Number Bond (double and single digits)

= 2 + 5 + 10   Regroup 15 into 5 and 10.

= 7 + 10

= **17**

4. Subtraction Number Bond (double and single digits)

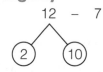

10 − 7 = 3

3 + 2 = **5**

5. Subtraction Number Bond (double digits)

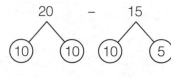

10 − 5 = 5

10 − 10 = 0

5 + 0 = **5**

Students should understand that multiplication is repeated addition and that division is the grouping of all items into equal sets.

1. Repeated Addition (Multiplication)

Mackenzie eats 2 rolls a day. How many rolls does she eat in 5 days?

$$2 + 2 + 2 + 2 + 2 = 10$$
$$5 \times 2 = 10$$

She eats **10** rolls in 5 days.

2. The Grouping Method (Division)

Mrs. Lee makes 14 sandwiches. She gives all the sandwiches equally to 7 friends. How many sandwiches does each friend receive?

$$14 \div 7 = 2$$

Each friend receives **2** sandwiches.

One of the basic but essential math skills students should acquire is to perform the 4 operations of whole numbers and fractions. Each of these methods is illustrated below.

1. The Adding-Without-Regrouping Method

```
  H  T  O
  3  2  1
+ 5  6  8
---------
  8  8  9
```

O: Ones

T: Tens

H: Hundreds

Since no regrouping is required, add the digits in each place value accordingly.

2. The Adding-by-Regrouping Method

```
   H  T  O
  ¹4  9  2
+  1  5  3
----------
   6  4  5
```

O: Ones

T: Tens

H: Hundreds

In this example, regroup 14 tens into 1 hundred 4 tens.

Singapore Math Level 1A & 1B

3. The Adding-by-Regrouping-Twice Method

$$\begin{array}{ccc} \text{H} & \text{T} & \text{O} \\ {}^1 2 & {}^1 8 & 6 \\ + \ 3 & 6 & 5 \\ \hline \mathbf{6} & \mathbf{5} & \mathbf{1} \end{array}$$

O: Ones
T: Tens
H: Hundreds

Regroup twice in this example.
First, regroup 11 ones into 1 ten 1 one.
Second, regroup 15 tens into 1 hundred 5 tens.

4. The Subtracting-Without-Regrouping Method

$$\begin{array}{ccc} \text{H} & \text{T} & \text{O} \\ 7 & 3 & 9 \\ - \ 3 & 2 & 5 \\ \hline \mathbf{4} & \mathbf{1} & \mathbf{4} \end{array}$$

O: Ones
T: Tens
H: Hundreds

Since no regrouping is required, subtract the digits in each place value accordingly.

5. The Subtracting-by-Regrouping Method

$$\begin{array}{ccc} \text{H} & \text{T} & \text{O} \\ 5 & {}^7 8 & {}^{11} 1 \\ - \ 2 & 4 & 7 \\ \hline \mathbf{3} & \mathbf{3} & \mathbf{4} \end{array}$$

O: Ones
T: Tens
H: Hundreds

In this example, students cannot subtract 7 ones from 1 one. So, regroup the tens and ones. Regroup 8 tens 1 one into 7 tens 11 ones.

6. The Subtracting-by-Regrouping-Twice Method

$$\begin{array}{ccc} \text{H} & \text{T} & \text{O} \\ {}^7 8 & {}^9 0 & {}^{10} 0 \\ - \ 5 & 9 & 3 \\ \hline \mathbf{2} & \mathbf{0} & \mathbf{7} \end{array}$$

O: Ones
T: Tens
H: Hundreds

In this example, students cannot subtract 3 ones from 0 ones and 9 tens from 0 tens. So, regroup the hundreds, tens, and ones. Regroup 8 hundreds into 7 hundreds 9 tens 10 ones.

7. The Multiplying-Without-Regrouping Method

$$\begin{array}{cc} \text{T} & \text{O} \\ 2 & 4 \\ \times & 2 \\ \hline \mathbf{4} & \mathbf{8} \end{array}$$

O: Ones
T: Tens

Since no regrouping is required, multiply the digit in each place value by the multiplier accordingly.

8. The Multiplying-With-Regrouping Method

$$\begin{array}{ccc} \text{H} & \text{T} & \text{O} \\ {}^1 3 & {}^2 4 & 9 \\ \times & & 3 \\ \hline \mathbf{1,} \ \mathbf{0} & \mathbf{4} & \mathbf{7} \end{array}$$

O: Ones
T: Tens
H: Hundreds

In this example, regroup 27 ones into 2 tens 7 ones, and 14 tens into 1 hundred 4 tens.

9. The Dividing-Without-Regrouping Method

$$\begin{array}{r} \mathbf{2\ 4\ 1} \\ 2\overline{)4\ 8\ 2} \\ \underline{-4} \\ 8 \\ \underline{-8} \\ 2 \\ \underline{-2} \\ 0 \end{array}$$

Since no regrouping is required, divide the digit in each place value by the divisor accordingly.

10. The Dividing-With-Regrouping Method

$$\begin{array}{r} \mathbf{1\ 6\ 6} \\ 5\overline{)8\ 3\ 0} \\ \underline{-5} \\ 3\ 3 \\ \underline{-3\ 0} \\ 3\ 0 \\ \underline{-3\ 0} \\ 0 \end{array}$$

In this example, regroup 3 hundreds into 30 tens and add 3 tens to make 33 tens. Regroup 3 tens into 30 ones.

11. The Addition-of-Fractions Method

$$\frac{1}{6} \times \frac{2}{2} + \frac{1}{4} \times \frac{3}{3} = \frac{2}{12} + \frac{3}{12} = \frac{5}{12}$$

Always remember to make the denominators common before adding the fractions.

12. The Subtraction-of-Fractions Method

$$\frac{1}{2} \times \frac{5}{5} - \frac{1}{5} \times \frac{2}{2} = \frac{5}{10} - \frac{2}{10} = \frac{3}{10}$$

Always remember to make the denominators common before subtracting the fractions.

13. The Multiplication-of-Fractions Method

$$\frac{\overset{1}{\cancel{3}}}{5} \times \frac{1}{\underset{3}{\cancel{9}}} = \frac{1}{15}$$

When the numerator and the denominator have a common multiple, reduce them to their lowest fractions.

14. The Division-of-Fractions Method

$$\frac{7}{9} \div \frac{1}{6} = \frac{7}{\underset{3}{\cancel{9}}} \times \frac{\overset{2}{\cancel{6}}}{1} = \frac{14}{3} = 4\frac{2}{3}$$

When dividing fractions, first change the division sign (÷) to the multiplication sign (×). Then, switch the numerator and denominator of the fraction on the right hand side. Multiply the fractions in the usual way.

Model drawing is an effective strategy used to solve math word problems. It is a visual representation of the information in word problems using bar units. By drawing the models, students will know of the variables given in the problem, the variables to find, and even the methods used to solve the problem.

Drawing models is also a versatile strategy. It can be applied to simple word problems involving addition, subtraction, multiplication, and division. It can also be applied to word problems related to fractions, decimals, percentage, and ratio.

The use of models also trains students to think in an algebraic manner, which uses symbols for representation.

The different types of bar models used to solve word problems are illustrated below.

1. The model that involves addition

Melissa has 50 blue beads and 20 red beads. How many beads does she have altogether?

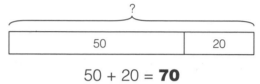

$$50 + 20 = \mathbf{70}$$

2. The model that involves subtraction

Ben and Andy have 90 toy cars. Andy has 60 toy cars. How many toy cars does Ben have?

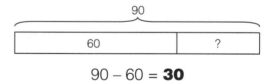

$$90 - 60 = \mathbf{30}$$

3. The model that involves comparison

Mr. Simons has 150 magazines and 110 books in his study. How many more magazines than books does he have?

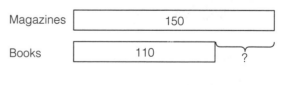

$$150 - 110 = \mathbf{40}$$

4. The model that involves two items with a difference

A pair of shoes costs $109. A leather bag costs $241 more than the pair of shoes. How much is the leather bag?

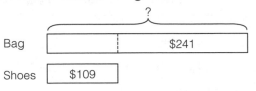

$$\$109 + \$241 = \textbf{\$350}$$

5. The model that involves multiples

Mrs. Drew buys 12 apples. She buys 3 times as many oranges as apples. She also buys 3 times as many cherries as oranges. How many pieces of fruit does she buy altogether?

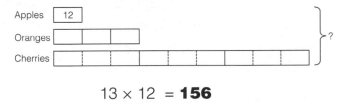

$$13 \times 12 = \textbf{156}$$

6. The model that involves multiples and difference

There are 15 students in Class A. There are 5 more students in Class B than in Class A. There are 3 times as many students in Class C than in Class A. How many students are there altogether in the three classes?

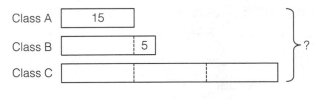

$$(5 \times 15) + 5 = \textbf{80}$$

7. The model that involves creating a whole

Ellen, Giselle, and Brenda bake 111 muffins. Giselle bakes twice as many muffins as Brenda. Ellen bakes 9 fewer muffins than Giselle. How many muffins does Ellen bake?

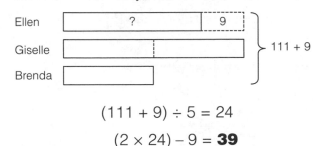

$$(111 + 9) \div 5 = 24$$
$$(2 \times 24) - 9 = \textbf{39}$$

8. The model that involves sharing

There are 183 tennis balls in Basket A and 97 tennis balls in Basket B. How many tennis balls must be transferred from Basket A to Basket B so that both baskets contain the same number of tennis balls?

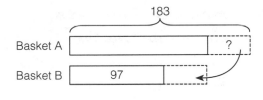

$$183 - 97 = 86$$
$$86 \div 2 = \textbf{43}$$

9. The model that involves fractions

George had 355 marbles. He lost $\frac{1}{5}$ of the marbles and gave $\frac{1}{4}$ of the remaining marbles to his brother. How many marbles did he have left?

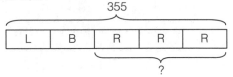

L: Lost
B: Brother
R: Remaining

$$5 \text{ parts} \rightarrow 355 \text{ marbles}$$
$$1 \text{ part} \rightarrow 355 \div 5 = 71 \text{ marbles}$$
$$3 \text{ parts} \rightarrow 3 \times 71 = \textbf{213} \text{ marbles}$$

Singapore Math Level 1A & 1B

10. The model that involves ratio

Aaron buys a tie and a belt. The prices of the tie and belt are in the ratio 2 : 5. If both items cost $539,

(a) what is the price of the tie?

(b) what is the price of the belt?

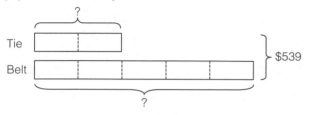

$539 ÷ 7 = $77

Tie (2 units) → 2 × $77 = **$154**

Belt (5 units) → 5 × $77 = **$385**

11. The model that involves comparison of fractions

Jack's height is $\frac{2}{3}$ of Leslie's height. Leslie's height is $\frac{3}{4}$ of Lindsay's height. If Lindsay is 160 cm tall, find Jack's height and Leslie's height.

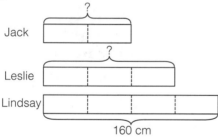

1 unit → 160 ÷ 4 = 40 cm

Leslie's height (3 units) → 3 × 40 = **120 cm**

Jack's height (2 units) → 2 × 40 = **80 cm**

Thinking skills and strategies are important in mathematical problem solving. These skills are applied when students think through the math problems to solve them. The following are some commonly used thinking skills and strategies applied in mathematical problem solving.

1. Comparing

Comparing is a form of thinking skill that students can apply to identify similarities and differences.

When comparing numbers, look carefully at each digit before deciding if a number is greater or less than the other. Students might also use a number line for comparison when there are more numbers.

Example:

3 is greater than 2 but smaller than 7.

2. Sequencing

A sequence shows the order of a series of numbers. *Sequencing* is a form of thinking skill that requires students to place numbers in a particular order. There are many terms in a sequence. The terms refer to the numbers in a sequence.

To place numbers in a correct order, students must first find a rule that generates the sequence. In a simple math sequence, students can either add or subtract to find the unknown terms in the sequence.

Example: Find the 7th term in the sequence below.

1,	4,	7,	10,	13,	16	?
1st term	2nd term	3rd term	4th term	5th term	6th term	7th term

Step 1: This sequence is in an increasing order.

Step 2: 4 − 1 = 3   7 − 4 = 3
The difference between two consecutive terms is 3.

Step 3: 16 + 3 = 19
The 7th term is **19**.

3. Visualization

Visualization is a problem solving strategy that can help students visualize a problem through the use of physical objects. Students will play a more active role in solving the problem by manipulating these objects.

The main advantage of using this strategy is the mobility of information in the process of solving the problem. When students make a wrong step in the process, they can retrace the step without erasing or canceling it.

The other advantage is that this strategy helps develop a better understanding of the problem or solution through visual objects or images. In this way, students will be better able to remember how to solve these types of problems.

Some of the commonly used objects for this strategy are toothpicks, straws, cards, strings, water, sand, pencils, paper, and dice.

4. Look for a Pattern

This strategy requires the use of observational and analytical skills. Students have to observe the given data to find a pattern in order to solve the problem. Math word problems that involve the use of this strategy usually have repeated numbers or patterns.

Example: Find the sum of all the numbers from 1 to 100.

Step 1: <u>Simplify the problem.</u>
Find the sum of 1, 2, 3, 4, 5, 6, 7, 8, 9, and 10.

Step 2: <u>Look for a pattern.</u>

$1 + 10 = 11$ $2 + 9 = 11$
$3 + 8 = 11$ $4 + 7 = 11$
$5 + 6 = 11$

Step 3: <u>Describe the pattern.</u>
When finding the sum of 1 to 10, add the first and last numbers to get a result of 11. Then, add the second and second last numbers to get the same result. The pattern continues until all the numbers from 1 to 10 are added. There will be 5 pairs of such results. Since each addition equals 11, the answer is then $5 \times 11 = 55$.

Step 4: <u>Use the pattern to find the answer.</u>
Since there are 5 pairs in the sum of 1 to 10, there should be ($10 \times 5 = 50$ pairs) in the sum of 1 to 100.

Note that the addition for each pair is not equal to 11 now. The addition for each pair is now ($1 + 100 = 101$).

$$50 \times 101 = 5050$$

The sum of all the numbers from 1 to 100 is **5,050**.

5. Working Backward

The strategy of working backward applies only to a specific type of math word problem. These word problems state the end result, and students are required to find the total number. In order to solve these word problems, students have to work backward by thinking through the correct sequence of events. The strategy of working backward allows students to use their logical reasoning and sequencing to find the answers.

Example: Sarah has a piece of ribbon. She cuts the ribbon into 4 equal parts. Each part is then cut into 3 smaller equal parts. If the length of each small part is 35 cm, how long is the piece of ribbon?

$$3 \times 35 = 105 \text{ cm}$$
$$4 \times 105 = 420 \text{ cm}$$

The piece of ribbon is **420 cm**.

6. The Before-After Concept

The *Before-After* concept lists all the relevant data before and after an event. Students can then compare the differences and eventually solve the problems. Usually, the Before-After concept and the mathematical model go hand in hand to solve math word problems. Note that the Before-After concept can be applied only to a certain type of math word problem, which trains students to think sequentially.

Example: Kelly has 4 times as much money as Joey. After Kelly uses some money to buy a tennis racquet, and Joey uses $30 to buy a pair of pants, Kelly has twice as much money as Joey. If Joey has $98 in the beginning,

(a) how much money does Kelly have in the end?

(b) how much money does Kelly spend on the tennis racquet?

Before

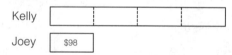

After

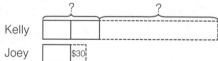

(a) $98 - $30 = $68
2 × $68 = $136
Kelly has **$136** in the end.

(b) 4 × $98 = $392
$392 − $136 = $256
Kelly spends **$256** on the tennis racquet.

7. Making Supposition

Making supposition is commonly known as "making an assumption." Students can use this strategy to solve certain types of math word problems. Making assumptions will eliminate some possibilities and simplifies the word problems by providing a boundary of values to work within.

Example: Mrs. Jackson bought 100 pieces of candy for all the students in her class. How many pieces of candy would each student receive if there were 25 students in her class?

In the above word problem, assume that each student received the same number of pieces. This eliminates the possibilities that some students would receive more than others due to good behavior, better results, or any other reason.

8. Representation of Problem

In problem solving, students often use representations in the solutions to show their understanding of the problems. Using representations also allow students to understand the mathematical concepts and relationships as well as to manipulate the information presented in the problems. Examples of representations are diagrams and lists or tables.

Diagrams allow students to consolidate or organize the information given in the problems. By drawing a diagram, students can see the problem clearly and solve it effectively.

A list or table can help students organize information that is useful for analysis. After analyzing, students can then see a pattern, which can be used to solve the problem.

9. Guess and Check

One of the most important and effective problem-solving techniques is *Guess and Check*. It is also known as *Trial and Error*. As the name suggests, students have to guess the answer to a problem and check if that guess is correct. If the guess is wrong, students will make another guess. This will continue until the guess is correct.

It is beneficial to keep a record of all the guesses and checks in a table. In addition, a *Comments* column can be included. This will enable students to analyze their guess (if it is too high or too low) and improve on the next guess. Be careful; this problem-solving technique can be tiresome without systematic or logical guesses.

Example: Jessica had 15 coins. Some of them were 10-cent coins and the rest were 5-cent coins. The total amount added up to $1.25. How many coins of each kind were there?

Use the guess-and-check method.

Number of 10¢ Coins	Value	Number of 5¢ Coins	Value	Total Number of Coins	Total Value
7	7 × 10¢ = 70¢	8	8 × 5¢ = 40¢	7 + 8 = 15	70¢ + 40¢ = 110¢ = $1.10
8	8 × 10¢ = 80¢	7	7 × 5¢ = 35¢	8 + 7 = 15	80¢ + 35¢ = 115¢ = $1.15
10	10 × 10¢ = 100¢	5	5 × 5¢ = 25¢	10 + 5 = 15	100¢ + 25¢ = 125¢ = $1.25

There were **ten** 10-cent coins and **five** 5-cent coins.

10. Restate the Problem

When solving challenging math problems, conventional methods may not be workable. Instead, restating the problem will enable students to see some challenging problems in a different light so that they can better understand them.

The strategy of restating the problem is to "say" the problem in a different and clearer way. However, students have to ensure that the main idea of the problem is not altered.

How do students restate a math problem?

First, read and understand the problem. Gather the given facts and unknowns. Note any condition(s) that have to be satisfied.

Next, restate the problem. Imagine narrating this problem to a friend. Present the given facts, unknown(s), and condition(s). Students may want to write the "revised" problem. Once the "revised" problem is analyzed, students should be able to think of an appropriate strategy to solve it.

11. Simplify the Problem

One of the commonly used strategies in mathematical problem solving is simplification of the problem. When a problem is simplified, it can be "broken down" into two or more smaller parts. Students can then solve the parts systematically to get to the final answer.

13

14

1A LEARNING OUTCOMES

Unit 1 Numbers 1–10
Students should be able to
- count numbers from 1 to 10.
- read and write numbers up to 10 in numerals and words.
- match numerals to words from 1 to 10.
- compare and arrange numbers in the correct order.
- complete number patterns.

Unit 2 Fun With Number Bonds
Students should be able to
- make number bonds.
- complete number bonds by filling in the missing parts.

Review 1
This review tests students' understanding of Units 1 & 2.

Unit 3 Adding Numbers up to 10
Students should be able to
- add by counting on.
- add using number bonds.
- make addition sentences.
- solve 1-step addition story problems.

Unit 4 Subtracting Numbers up to 10
Students should be able to
- subtract by crossing out, counting on, counting backward, and using number bonds.
- make subtraction sentences.
- make a series of addition and subtraction sentences.
- solve 1-step subtraction story problems.

Review 2
This review tests students' understanding of Units 3 & 4.

Unit 5 Shapes and Patterns
Students should be able to
- identify and recognize squares, rectangles, circles, and triangles.
- complete the patterns.

Unit 6 Ordinal Numbers
Students should be able to
- understand ordinal numbers, like first, second, third, fourth, etc.
- use symbols, like 1st, 2nd, 3rd, 4th, etc.
- understand the left and right positions.

Review 3
This review tests students' understanding of Units 5 & 6.

Unit 7 Numbers 1–20
Students should be able to
- know numbers from 1 to 20 in numerals and words.
- know the place value up to 20.
- compare and arrange numbers up to 20.
- complete number patterns.

Unit 8 Adding and Subtracting Numbers up to 20
Students should be able to
- add and subtract numbers up to 20.
- use number bonds to make a 10 when adding and subtracting numbers.
- solve 1-step story sums related to addition and subtraction.

Unit 9 Length
Students should be able to
- measure and compare length.
- understand the meaning of words like *tall, taller, tallest, short, shorter, shortest, long, longer, longest, high, higher,* and *highest.*
- understand the left and right positions.

Final Review
This review is an excellent assessment of students' understanding of all the topics inthe first half of this book.

FORMULA SHEET

Unit 1 Numbers 1–10

Numerals	Words	Pictorial Representation
1	one	○
2	two	○○
3	three	○○○
4	four	○○○○
5	five	○○○○○
6	six	○○○○○○
7	seven	○○○○○○○
8	eight	○○○○○○○○
9	nine	○○○○○○○○○
10	ten	○○○○○○○○○○

Comparing Numbers
- Count the number in each set.
- When there are equal numbers in both sets, use the word *same* to describe them.
- When one set is more than another, use the words *more* or *greater* to describe it.
- When one set is less than another, use the words *fewer* or *smaller* to describe it.

To find a number that is "more than," count on to find the answer.
Example: What is 1 more than 2?

1, 2, 3
1 more than 2 is **3**.

To find a number that is "less than," count backward to find the answer.
Example: What is 1 less than 9?

1, 2, 3, 4, 5, 6, 7, 8, 9
1 less than 9 is **8**.

Number Patterns
- To complete a number pattern, be familiar with the numbers 1 to 10 in the correct order.
- Take note of the order in the number pattern when working to complete it.

1, 2, 3, 4, 5, 6, 7, 8, 9, 10 (increasing order)

10, 9, 8, 7, 6, 5, 4, 3, 2, 1 (decreasing order)

Unit 2 Fun With Number Bonds
2 small numbers can make 1 big number.
Examples: **2** and **4** make 6.
4 and **5** make 9.

We can interpret the 2 number sentences as number bonds.

For each number bond, the circle on the left is known as the whole. The 2 circles on the right are known as the parts.

Number bonds can also be broken down into 3 parts.

Number bonds are useful because they can be broken down into smaller numbers for easy addition or subtraction.

Unit 3 Adding Numbers up to 10
To add is to find the total number of items.

Some keywords used in addition problems are *add, plus, more than, sum, altogether, in all,* and *total*.

There are two ways to add numbers:
- counting on
- number bonds

Below is an addition grid that can be useful for solving addition problems.

+	0	1	2	3	4	5	6	7	8	9	10
0	0	1	2	3	4	5	6	7	8	9	10
1	1	2	3	4	5	6	7	8	9	10	
2	2	3	4	5	6	7	8	9	10		
3	3	4	5	6	7	8	9	10			
4	4	5	6	7	8	9	10				
5	5	6	7	8	9	10					
6	6	7	8	9	10						
7	7	8	9	10							
8	8	9	10								
9	9	10									
10	10										

Singapore Math Level 1A & 1B

Unit 4 Subtracting Numbers up to 10

To subtract is to find the number of items left after removing some of them.

Some keywords used in subtraction problems are *subtract, minus, less than,* and *take away*.

There are four ways to subtract numbers:
- crossing out
- counting on
- counting backward
- number bonds

Below is a subtraction grid that can be useful for solving subtraction problems.

–	0	1	2	3	4	5	6	7	8	9	10
10	10	9	8	7	6	5	4	3	2	1	0
9	9	8	7	6	5	4	3	2	1	0	
8	8	7	6	5	4	3	2	1	0		
7	7	6	5	4	3	2	1	0			
6	6	5	4	3	2	1	0				
5	5	4	3	2	1	0					
4	4	3	2	1	0						
3	3	2	1	0							
2	2	1	0								
1	1	0									
0	0										

Unit 5 Shapes and Patterns

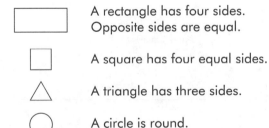

A rectangle has four sides.
Opposite sides are equal.

A square has four equal sides.

A triangle has three sides.

A circle is round.

We can see changes in size, shape, color, and position in a pattern.

When completing a pattern, be observant to see how the pattern repeats.

Unit 6 Ordinal Numbers

1st	2nd	3rd	4th	5th
first	second	third	fourth	fifth

6th	7th	8th	9th	10th
sixth	seventh	eighth	ninth	tenth

before: the position in front
Example: 4th is before 5th.

after: the position behind
Example: 9th is after 8th.

between: in the center of 2 items
Example: 6th is between 5th and 7th.

We can count things from the left or right positions.

Unit 7 Numbers 1–20

Numerals	Words	Pictorial Representation
11	eleven	
12	twelve	
13	thirteen	
14	fourteen	
15	fifteen	
16	sixteen	
17	seventeen	
18	eighteen	
19	nineteen	
20	twenty	

Place Value
Group numbers greater than 10 into tens and ones.
Example: 18 = **1** ten **8** ones

Number Patterns
When completing number patterns,
1. see if the number pattern is in an increasing or a decreasing order.
2. observe the difference between each number.
3. add or subtract to get the next number.

Number Order
When arranging numbers in order, see if the numbers start with the smallest or the largest.

Unit 8 Adding and Subtracting Numbers up to 20

There are 2 ways to add numbers up to 20:
- make a group of 10.
- regroup one of the addends into tens and ones using number bonds.

To subtract numbers up to 20, regroup the minuend into tens and ones using number bonds.

Unit 9 Length

When measuring length, make sure that objects are placed on the same starting line.
The measurement will be accurate, and it is easier to identify the longest or the shortest length.

Singapore Math Level 1A & 1B

Unit 1: NUMBERS 1–10

Examples:

1. Count the number of toy cars. Write the number and the word.

Number: **7**   Word: **seven**

2. Compare the numbers below.

          (6)   (8)

    6 is smaller than **8**.

    8 is greater than **6**.

3. Complete the number pattern.

          3, 4, ___, ___, 7, 8

    3, 4, **5**, **6**, 7, 8

4. What is 1 less than 10?

    9 is 1 less than 10.

Singapore Math Level 1A & 1B

Count the items, and write the numbers on the lines.

1.

_____ ribbons

2.

_____ cats

3.

_____ cars

4.

_____ bus

5.

_____ dolphins

6.

_____ bicycles

7.

_____ flowers

8.

_____ birds

9.

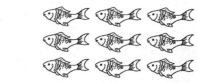

_____ fish

10.

_____ shoes

Singapore Math Level 1A & 1B

Read each sentence carefully. Complete the drawing.

11. The cat has 1 tail.

14. The bicycle has 2 wheels.

12. There are 3 flowers in the vase.

15. The table has 4 legs.

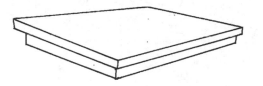

13. There are 6 oranges on this plate.

Singapore Math Level 1A & 1B

Count the number of each object. Circle the correct word.

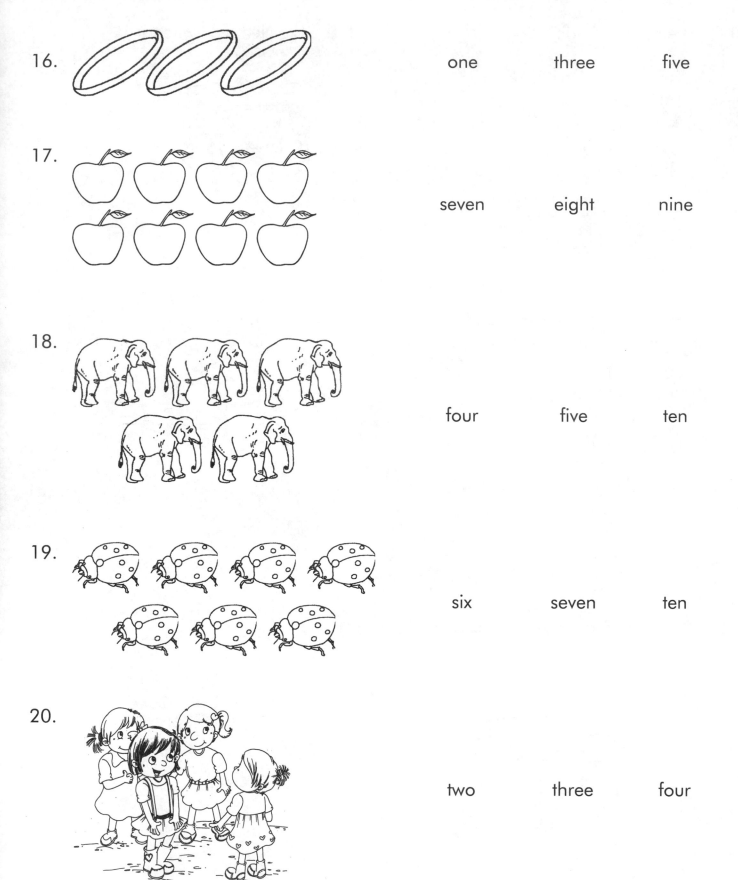

16.   one   three   five

17.   seven   eight   nine

18.   four   five   ten

19.   six   seven   ten

20.   two   three   four

21. Match each car to the correct garage.

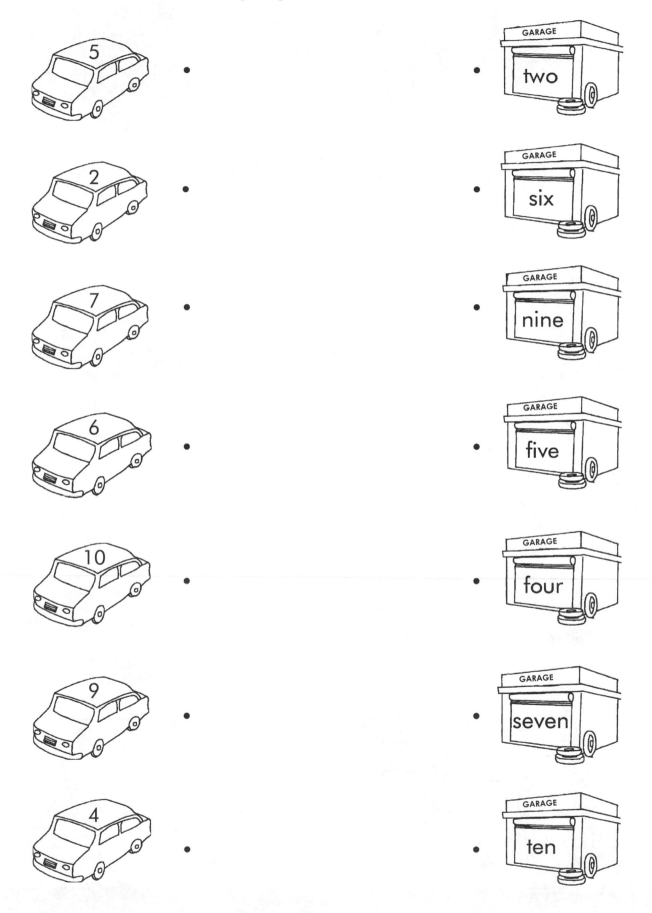

Singapore Math Level 1A & 1B

Draw pictures in each box to show the correct number of objects.

22.	3 apples
23.	6 balls
24.	8 fish
25.	7 stars
26.	10 pencils

Singapore Math Level 1A & 1B

Fill in each blank with the correct word.

27.

more	fewer

There are _____ boys than bicycles.

There are _____ bicycles than boys.

28.

trees	flowers

There are more _____ than _____ .

There are fewer _____ than _____ .

29.

more	fewer

There are _____ oranges than apples.

There are _____ apples than oranges.

Singapore Math Level 1A & 1B

30.

more	fewer

There are _____ shirts than skirts.

There are _____ skirts than shirts.

31.

boys	girls

There are more _____ than _____.

There are fewer _____ than _____.

Singapore Math Level 1A & 1B

Circle the smaller number in each pair.

32.   6   4   35.   7   9

33.   10   8   36.   5   2

34.   1   3

Color the larger number in each pair.

37. 

38.

39. 

40.

41. 8   1

Singapore Math Level 1A & 1B

Complete each number pattern.

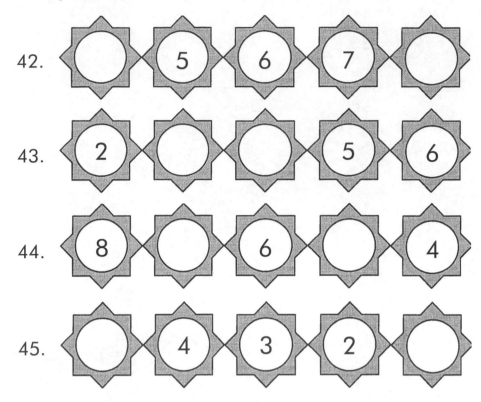

42. ☐ 5 6 7 ☐

43. 2 ☐ ☐ 5 6

44. 8 ☐ 6 ☐ 4

45. ☐ 4 3 2 ☐

Fill in each blank with the correct answer.

46. 1 more than 2 is _____.

47. 1 more than 7 is _____.

48. 1 more than 3 is _____.

49. 1 more than 1 is _____.

50. _____ is 1 more than 4.

51. _____ is 1 more than 8.

52. _____ is 1 more than 5.

53. _____ is 1 more than 2.

54. 1 less than 7 is _____.

55. 1 less than 4 is _____.

56. 1 less than 8 is _____.

57. 1 less than 2 is _____.

58. _____ is 1 less than 3.

59. _____ is 1 less than 6.

60. _____ is 1 less than 9.

61. _____ is 1 less than 5.

62. Benjamin can walk from his school to the library. Fill in each blank with the correct number written as either a numeral or a word.

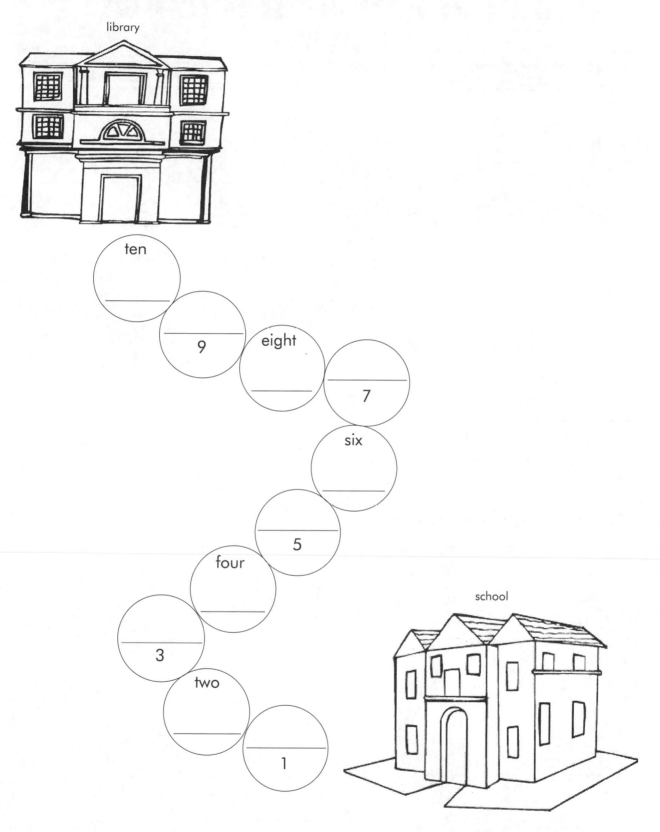

The library is _____ steps away from the school.

Singapore Math Level 1A & 1B

Examples:

1.

Make a number bond using the above picture.

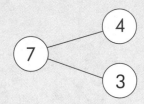

2. Make number bonds for the number 8.

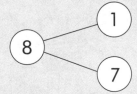

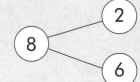

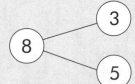

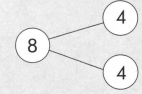

Singapore Math Level 1A & 1B

Look at each picture carefully. Then, complete the number bond beside it.

1.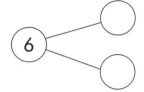

2.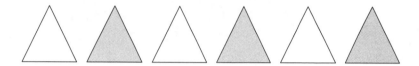

3.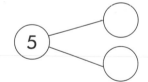

4.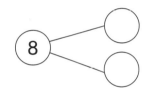

5.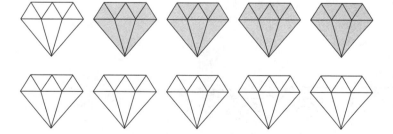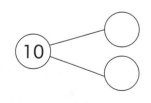

Singapore Math Level 1A & 1B

Study each picture carefully. Fill in the missing numbers. The first one has been done for you.

6.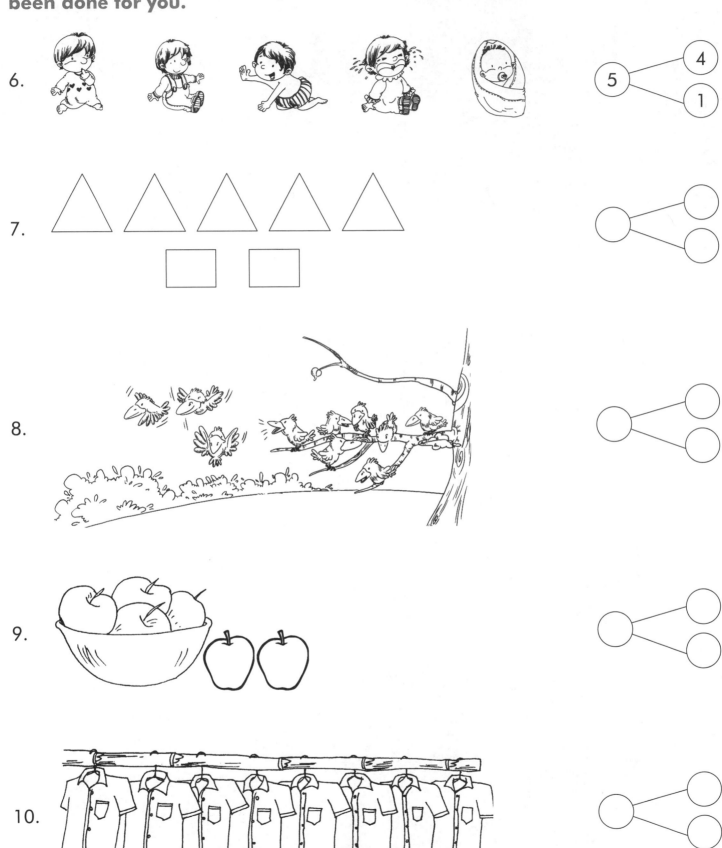

Singapore Math Level 1A & 1B

11.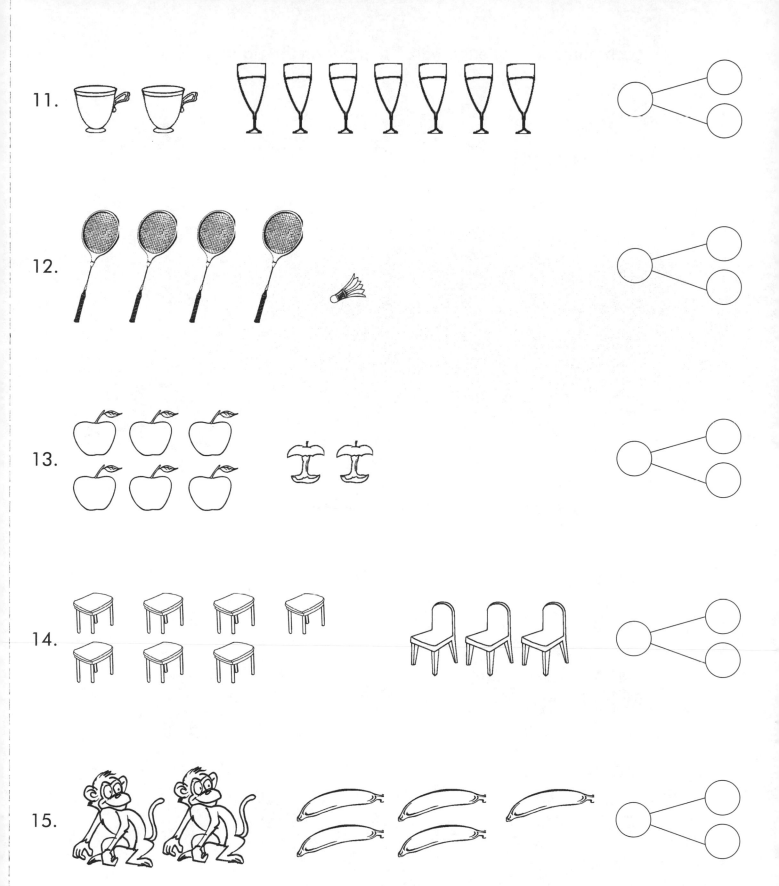

12.

13.

14.

15.

16. Match each number on the left with a number on the right to make 7.

17. Match each number on the left with a number on the right to make 8.

Singapore Math Level 1A & 1B

18. Match each number on the left with a number on the right to make 9.

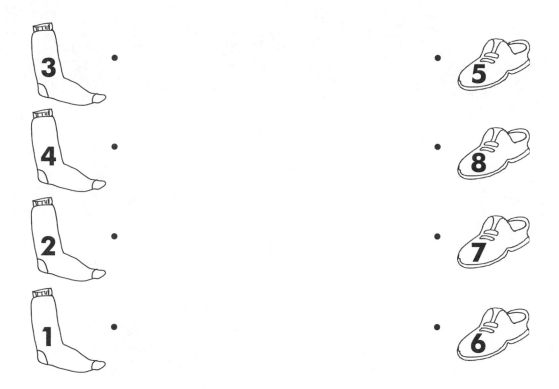

19. Match each number on the left with a number on the right to make 10.

Singapore Math Level 1A & 1B

Fill in the missing number in each number bond.

20.

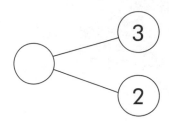

21.

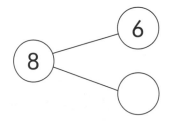

22.

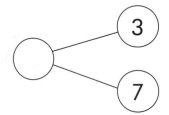

23.

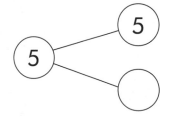

24.

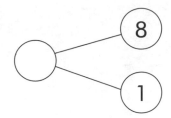

25.

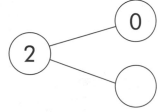

26.

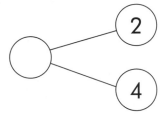

27.

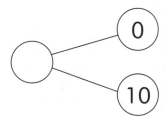

Singapore Math Level 1A & 1B

REVIEW 1

Count the objects in each picture. Write the correct number on the line.

1.

_____ wheels

2.

_____ buses

3.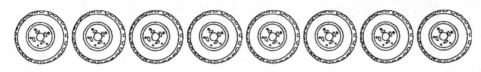

_____ bottles

Look at each picture carefully. Fill in the missing parts in each number bond.

4.

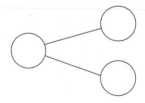

5.

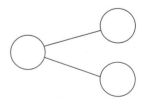

Singapore Math Level 1A & 1B

Complete the pictures to show the correct numbers.

6. The chair has 4 legs.

7. There are 7 apples on the tree.

8. Match each number on the left with a number on the right to make 6.

 •

•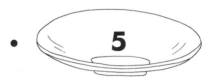

 •

•

 •

•

Singapore Math Level 1A & 1B

Count the number of objects in each group. Circle the correct word.

9. 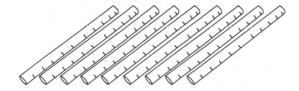   six   ten   eight   nine

10.    five   three   four   two

11.    seven   six   zero   eight

Fill in each blank with the correct word from the box.

12.

more	fewer

There are _____ books than pencils.

There are _____ pencils than books.

Singapore Math Level 1A & 1B

13.

ladybugs	leaves

There are more _____ than _____.

There are fewer _____ than _____.

14. Circle the larger number.

          7   9

15. Circle the smaller number.

          3   5

16. Complete the number pattern.

      _____, _____, 7, 8, 9

17. 1 more than 9 is _____.

Fill in the missing number in each number bond.

18.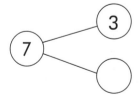

20.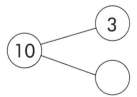

19.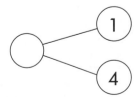

Singapore Math Level 1A & 1B

Unit 3: ADDING NUMBERS UP TO 10

Examples:

1. What number is 4 more than 6?

6, 7, 8, 9, 10

10 is 4 more than 6.

2. Some students are using 6 computers in a computer lab.
   There are 2 computers that are not being used.
   How many computers are there altogether in the computer lab?

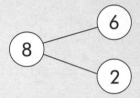

There are **8** computers altogether in the computer lab.

Complete the addition sentences by counting on.

1.

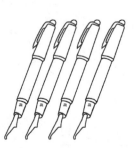 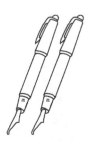

4 + _____ = _____

Singapore Math Level 1A & 1B

2.

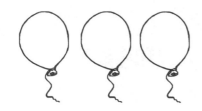

$$3 + \underline{\hspace{2em}} = \underline{\hspace{2em}}$$

3.

$$6 + \underline{\hspace{2em}} = \underline{\hspace{2em}}$$

4.

$$2 + \underline{\hspace{2em}} = \underline{\hspace{2em}}$$

5.

$$5 + \underline{\hspace{2em}} = \underline{\hspace{2em}}$$

Singapore Math Level 1A & 1B

Look at each picture carefully. Write the addition sentence on the lines.

6. ★ ★   ★
    ★ ★   ★ ★   _____ + _____ = _____

7.   ★   ★ ★
    ★ ★   ★ ★ ★   _____ + _____ = _____
               ★ ★

8. ★ ★   ★ ★
    　★   　★   _____ + _____ = _____
    ★ ★   ★ ★

9.   ★ ★
       ★   ★ ★   _____ + _____ = _____
                ★ ★

10. ★ ★   ★ ★
    ★ ★   ★ ★   _____ + _____ = _____
               ★ ★

11.   ★ ★
    ★ ★   　★   _____ + _____ = _____
               ★ ★

Fill in each blank with the correct answer.

12. 2 more than 3   =   3   +   2   =   _____

13. 4 more than 5   =   _____   +   _____   =   _____

14. 3 more than 6   =   _____   +   _____   =   _____

15. 1 more than 2   =   _____   +   _____   =   _____

16. 5 more than 0   =   _____   +   _____   =   _____

Singapore Math Level 1A & 1B

Study the pictures below. Fill in the blanks with the correct answers. Use number bonds to help you.

17.

_____ girls are performing onstage.

18.

There are _____ penguins in all.

19.

There are _____ boys altogether.

20.

There are _____ flowers altogether.

21.

There are _____ rabbits altogether.

Singapore Math Level 1A & 1B

Fill in each blank with the correct answer.

22.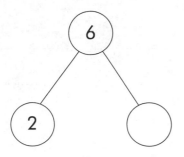

27.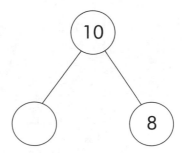

23.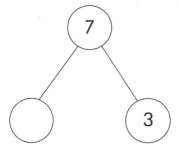

28.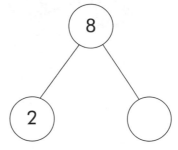

24.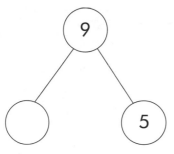

29.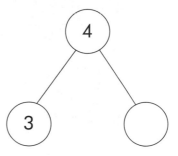

25.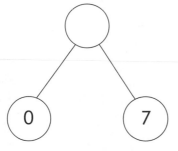

30.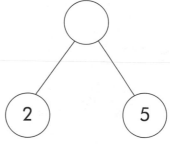

26.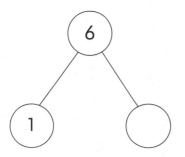

31.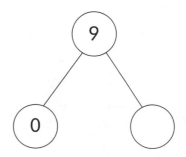

Singapore Math Level 1A & 1B

Color the correct rectangle to match the number in the circle.

32. ⑨ | 2 + 6 | | 3 + 7 | | 4 + 5 | | 5 + 2 |

33. ⑦ | 1 + 5 | | 4 + 4 | | 7 + 0 | | 8 + 1 |

34. ⑤ | 3 + 2 | | 2 + 4 | | 5 + 2 | | 1 + 7 |

35. ⑥ | 3 + 1 | | 3 + 2 | | 3 + 3 | | 1 + 4 |

36. ④ | 4 + 1 | | 3 + 4 | | 2 + 1 | | 0 + 4 |

Fill in each blank with the correct answer.

37. ____ + 6 = 9

38. 1 + ____ = 8

39. 3 + ____ = 5

40. ____ + 4 = 8

41. 5 + ____ = 6

42. ____ + 7 = 9

43. ____ + 6 = 10

44. ____ + 3 = 3

45. 3 + ____ = 7

46. ____ + 2 = 2

Complete the addition stories by filling in the blanks.

47.

□ ○ □ = □

_____ zebras are eating the grass.

_____ zebras are not eating the grass.

There are _____ zebras altogether.

48.

□ ○ □ = □

There are _____ tables.

There are _____ chairs.

There are _____ pieces of furniture altogether.

49.

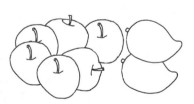

□ ○ □ = □

There are _____ apples.

There are _____ mangoes.

There are _____ pieces of fruit altogether.

Singapore Math Level 1A & 1B

Read each story problem. Then, fill in the blanks.

50. There are 4 people standing in a room. 5 people are sitting in the same room. How many people are in the room altogether?

There are _____ people in the room altogether.

51. 2 boys are drinking in the cafeteria. 5 boys are eating in the cafeteria. How many boys are in the cafeteria altogether?

There are _____ boys in the cafeteria altogether.

52. Sean has 3 toy cars. He has 6 toy airplanes. How many toys does he have in all?

He has _____ toys in all.

Singapore Math Level 1A & 1B

How many are there altogether? Write the correct answers on the lines.

53.

_____ + _____ = _____

There are _____ rabbits altogether.

54. There are 5 socks in the washing machine. There are 2 socks in the laundry basket. How many socks are there altogether?

_____

There are _____ socks altogether.

55. Andy borrows 5 books from the library. He borrows 1 more book from his friend. How many books does he borrow altogether?

_____

He borrows _____ books altogether.

Singapore Math Level 1A & 1B

56. There are 4 spoons on the table. There are 6 spoons in the sink. How many spoons are there altogether?

_____

There are _____ spoons altogether.

57. There are 6 plates in the dishwasher. There is 1 plate on the table. How many plates are there altogether?

_____

There are _____ plates altogether.

Unit 4: SUBTRACTING NUMBERS UP TO 10

Examples:

1. What number is 3 less than 6?

    $$6 - 3 = 3$$

    3 is 3 less than 6.

2. Subtract 2 from 7.

    7,   6,   5

    $7 - 2 = $ **5**

3. Subtract 4 from 9.

    9,   8,   7,   6,   5

    $9 - 4 = $ **5**

4. James has 10 postcards.
    He sends 3 postcards to his friend.
    How many postcards does he have left?

    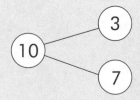

    He has **7** postcards left.

Singapore Math Level 1A & 1B

Cross out the correct number of objects in each set. Fill in each blank with the correct answer.

1.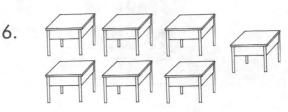

   5 − 2 = _____

2.

   10 − 6 = _____

3.

   8 − 3 = _____

4.

   9 − 4 = _____

5.

   6 − 5 = _____

6.

   7 − 1 = _____

7.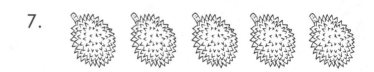

   5 − 0 = _____

8.

   8 − 5 = _____

9.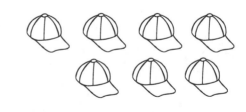

   7 − 3 = _____

10.

    10 − 7 = _____

Singapore Math Level 1A & 1B

How many are left? Write the correct answers on the lines.

11.

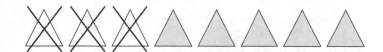

$8 - 3 =$ _____

There are _____ triangles left.

12.

_____ – _____ = _____

There are _____ books left.

13.

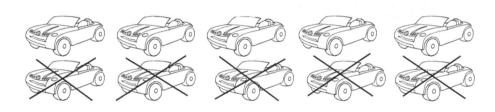

_____ – _____ = _____

There are _____ toy cars left.

14.

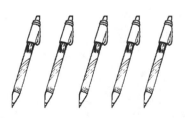

_____ – _____ = _____

There are _____ pens left.

Singapore Math Level 1A & 1B

15.

_____ – _____ = _____

There are _____ butterflies left.

Solve these subtraction problems by counting on. Use the numbers in the box below to help you count.

1	2	3	4	5	6	7	8	9	10

16. 9 – 3 = _____   19. 8 – 6 = _____

17. 6 – 1 = _____   20. 10 – 4 = _____

18. 3 – 2 = _____

Solve these subtraction problems by counting backward. Use the numbers in the box below to help you count.

1	2	3	4	5	6	7	8	9	10

21. 5 – 2 = _____   24. 9 – 2 = _____

22. 10 – 5 = _____   25. 4 – 3 = _____

23. 7 – 1 = _____

Singapore Math Level 1A & 1B

Fill in the missing numbers in each number bond to show the parts and the whole.

26.

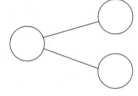

27.

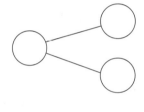

28.

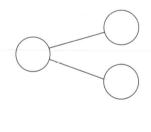

29.

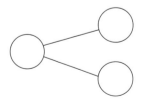

30.

Singapore Math Level 1A & 1B

Study the pictures below. Fill in the blanks with the correct answers.

31.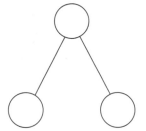

Diego has _____ toy car left.

32.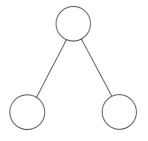

Mr. Johnson has _____ telephones left.

33.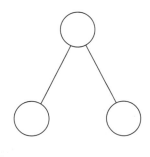

_____ trains remained at the station.

34.

Ella has _____ starfish left.

Singapore Math Level 1A & 1B

35.

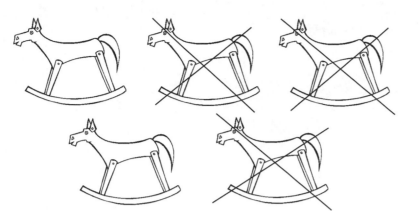

There are _____ rocking horses left.

36. Match each mouse to the correct piece of cheese.

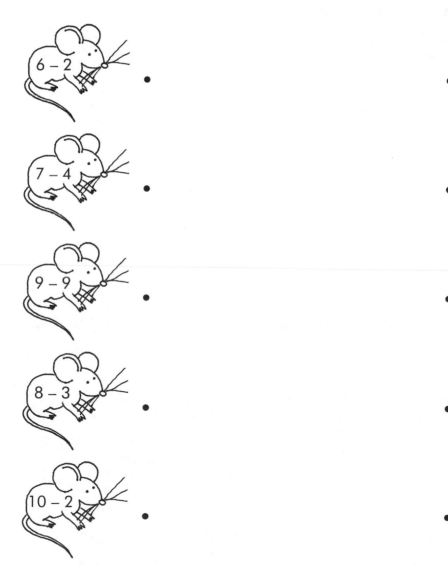

8

5

0

4

3

Fill in each blank with the correct answer.

37. 8 – 4 = _____

38. 2 – 0 = _____

39. 7 – 6 = _____

40. 9 – 2 = _____

41. 5 – 1 = _____

42. 6 – 6 = _____

43. 4 – 3 = _____

44. 10 – 3 = _____

45. 8 – 2 = _____

46. 10 – 5 = _____

Use the pictures to write subtraction stories.

47. There are _____ girls.

_____ girls have short hair.

8 （ – ） 3 = ☐

_____ girls have long hair.

48. There are _____ triangles and rectangles.

There are _____ triangles.

☐ （ – ） 4 = ☐

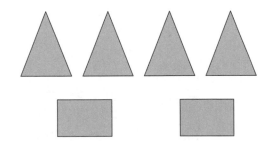

There are _____ rectangles.

Singapore Math Level 1A & 1B

49. There are _____ cats.

_____ cats have ribbons.

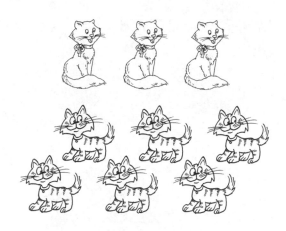

□ ─ 3 = □

_____ cats have no ribbons.

50. There are _____ boys.

_____ boys wear hats.

□ ─ 2 = □

_____ boys do not wear hats.

Read each story problem, and then, fill in the blanks. Show your work in the space below.

51. There are 6 packages of crackers. Amanda eats 2 packages. How many packages are left?

_____ packages of crackers are left.

52. Malia buys 10 red and green apples. 3 of the apples are green. How many red apples are there?

There are _____ red apples.

53. Ben has 5 toy airplanes. He gives 3 toy airplanes to his cousin. How many toy airplanes does Ben have left?

Ben has _____ toy airplanes left.

Study each set of pictures carefully. Then, write a series of addition and subtraction sentences.

54.

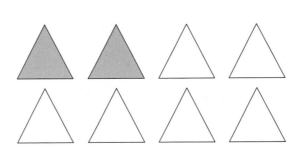

□ ○ □ = □   □ ○ □ = □

□ ○ □ = □   □ ○ □ = □

Singapore Math Level 1A & 1B

55.

□ ○ □ = □   □ ○ □ = □

□ ○ □ = □   □ ○ □ = □

56.

□ ○ □ = □   □ ○ □ = □

□ ○ □ = □   □ ○ □ = □

REVIEW 2

Study the pictures carefully. Fill in the blanks with the correct answers.

1.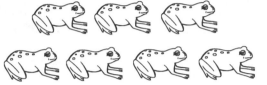

    $3 + \underline{\hspace{1cm}} = \underline{\hspace{1cm}}$

2.

    $\underline{\hspace{1cm}} + \underline{\hspace{1cm}} = \underline{\hspace{1cm}}$

Cross out the correct number of objects in each set. Fill in the blanks with the correct answers.

3.

    $4 - 4 = \underline{\hspace{1cm}}$

4.

    $8 - 6 = \underline{\hspace{1cm}}$

Study the pictures below. Fill in the blanks with the correct answers.

5.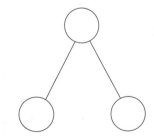

    $8 - 3 = \underline{\hspace{1cm}}$

Singapore Math Level 1A & 1B

6.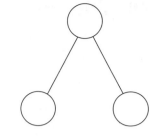

_____ − _____ = _____

7.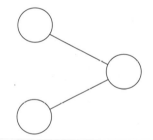

_____ − _____ = _____

8.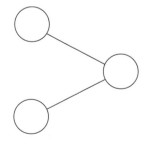

_____ + _____ = _____

9.

_____ + _____ = _____

Fill in the missing numbers.

10. $4 + 3 = $ _____

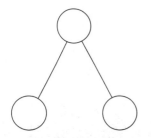

12. _____ $- 0 = 7$

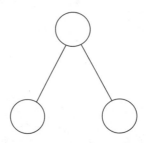

11. $5 + $ _____ $= 5$

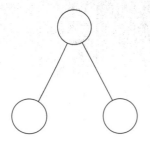

13. $10 - $ _____ $= 1$

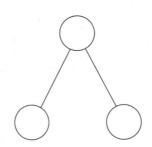

Write the correct answers on the lines.

14.

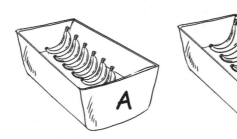

There are _____ bananas in Basket A.

There are _____ bananas in Basket B.

□ ○ □ = □

There are _____ bananas altogether.

Singapore Math Level 1A & 1B

15.

There are _____ cats.

_____ cats have short tails.

$$\square \bigcirc \square = \square$$

_____ cats have long tails.

Write 2 addition and 2 subtraction sentences for the picture.

16.

$$\square \bigcirc \square = \square \qquad \square \bigcirc \square = \square$$

$$\square \bigcirc \square = \square \qquad \square \bigcirc \square = \square$$

Read each story problem. Then, fill in the blank. Show your work in the space below.

17. Nadia has 7 dolls. Her mother gives her 2 more dolls on her birthday. How many dolls does she have in all?

    She has _____ dolls in all.

18. Mackenzie saves $10. She buys a present for $5. How much money does she have left?

    She has _____ left.

Singapore Math Level 1A & 1B

19. Troy gives 4 toy planes to his brother. He has 2 toy planes left. How many toy planes does he have at first?

He has _____ toy planes at first.

20. Lin needs 8 stars to win a prize. She has collected 3 stars. How many more stars does she need to collect?

She needs to collect _____ more stars.

Singapore Math Level 1A & 1B

Unit 5: SHAPES AND PATTERNS

Study the pictures below. Fill in each blank with the correct answer from the box.

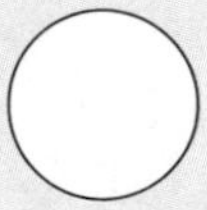

| square | triangle | circle | rectangle |

1. 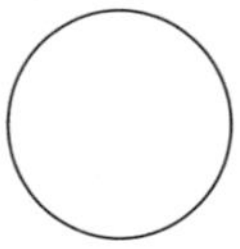 ◯

    _____

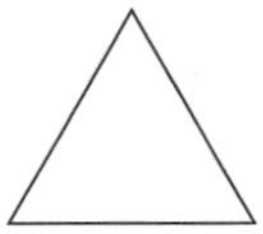

2. 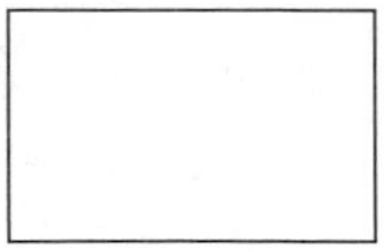 ▭

    _____

3. △

    _____

4. ☐

    _____

Singapore Math Level 1A & 1B

Match each shape to its correct name.

5.  •   • square

6.  •   • triangle

7. •   • circle

8.  •   • rectangle

Color the 2 objects in each set that are exactly the same.

9.

10.

11.

12.

Singapore Math Level 1A & 1B

13. Write the number 1 on all rectangles, 2 on all triangles, 3 on all squares, and 4 on all circles.

Singapore Math Level 1A & 1B

14. Make your own picture using the following shapes.

    (a)   3 rectangles   (c)   2 squares

    (b)   2 circles   (d)   1 triangle

15. Color the shapes using the key below.

        square = blue   circle = yellow

        rectangle = red   triangle = green

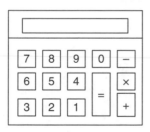 

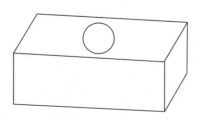 

Singapore Math Level 1A & 1B

Complete the patterns.

16. 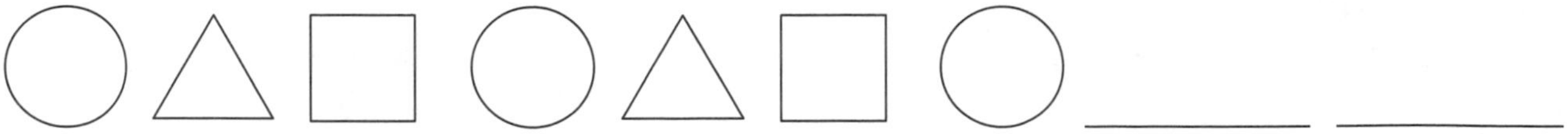 ○ △ □ ○ △ □ ○ _____ _____

17. 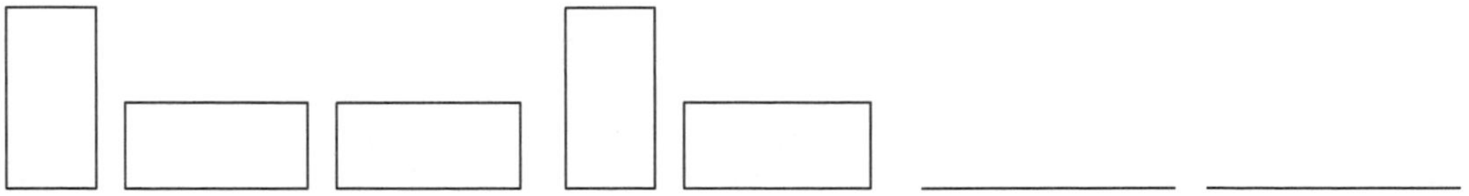 [rectangles pattern] _____ _____

18. 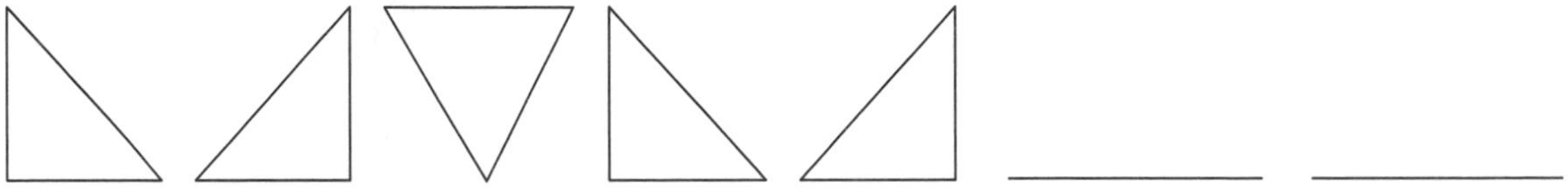 [triangles pattern] _____ _____

19. 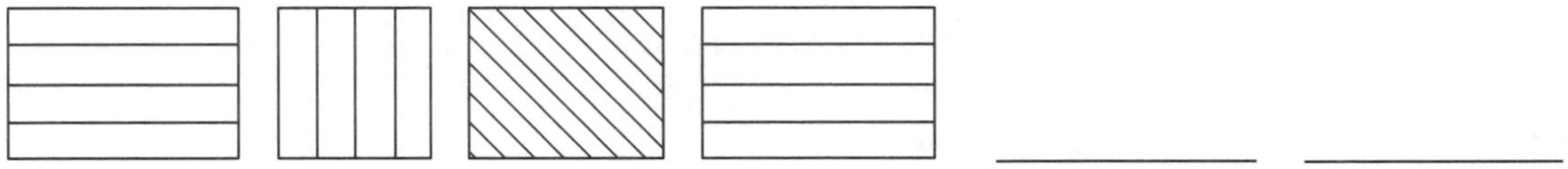 [squares pattern] _____ _____

20. 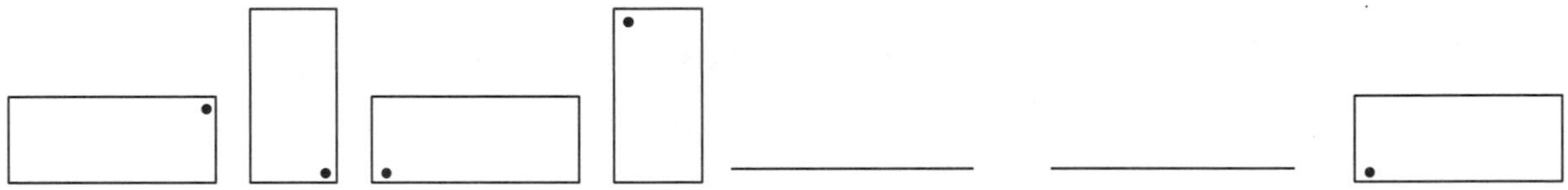 [rectangles with dots pattern] _____ _____ [rectangle]

21.  ○ [rectangle] [square] _____ [rectangle] [square] ○

22. 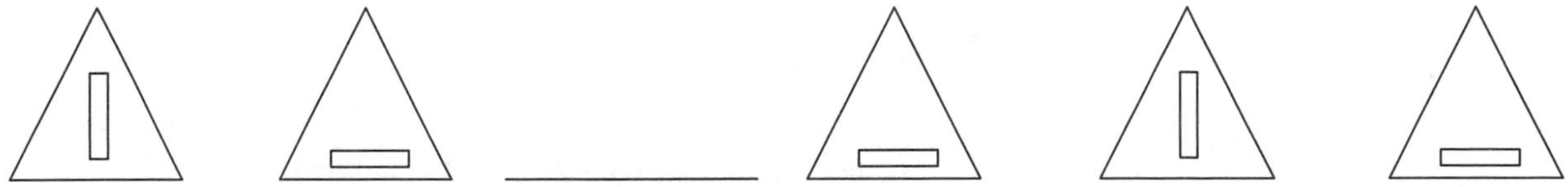 [triangles pattern] _____ [triangle] [triangle] [triangle]

23. 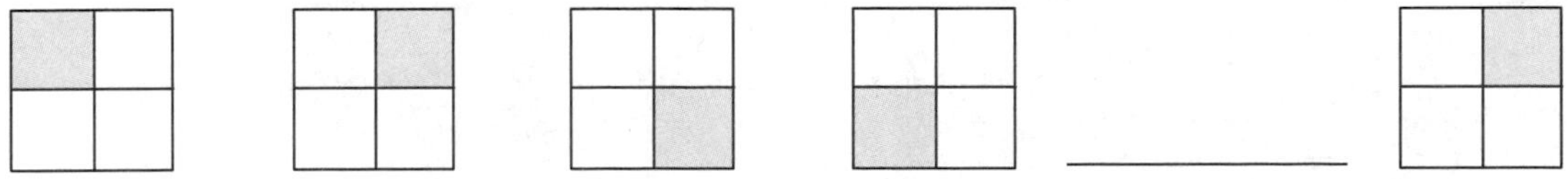 [four-square grids pattern] _____ [grid]

Singapore Math Level 1A & 1B

24.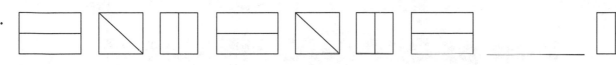

What is the next shape in the pattern? Draw an X beside the correct answer.

25.

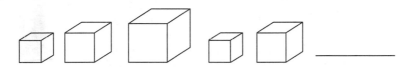

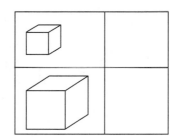

26.

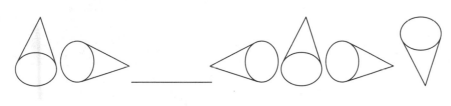

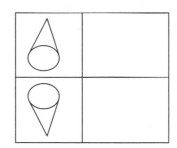

27.

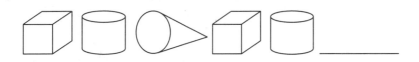

28.

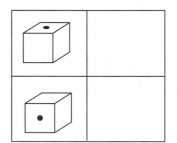

Singapore Math Level 1A & 1B

Unit 6: ORDINAL NUMBERS

Examples:

Look carefully at the picture below. Use it to answer the questions.

Angie   Antonio   James   Maria   Grace   Calvin   Riley   Miley

1st

1. Who is just before Maria?   **James**

2. Who is just after Grace?   **Calvin**

3. Who is between Angie and James?   **Antonio**

4. Who is next to Miley?   **Riley**

5. Who is farthest from the left?   **Miley**

6. Who is 5th from the left?   **Grace**

7. Who is sixth from the right?   **James**

8. Who is third from the right?   **Calvin**

Singapore Math Level 1A & 1B

Color the correct item in each set of pictures.

1. The fourth lamb

1st

2. The sixth carrot

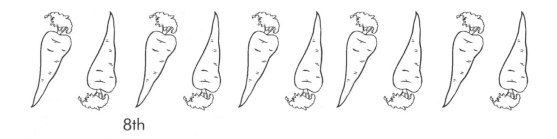

8th

3. The second mushroom

4th

4. The eighth party hat

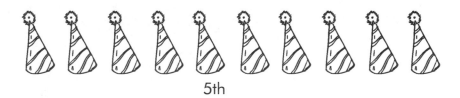

5th

5. The seventh present

2nd

Singapore Math Level 1A & 1B

Match each strawberry on the left to the correct pie on the right.

6. •   •  sixth

7. •   •  fourth

8. •   •  ninth

9. •   •  second

10. •   •  fifth

11. •   •  first

12. •   •  seventh

13. •   •  tenth

14. •   •  third

15. •   •  eighth

Singapore Math Level 1A & 1B

Fill in each blank with the correct word.

16. Tom is _____ in the line.

17. The _____ child in line is Sanja.

18. Luke is just before _____.

19. Dante is just after _____.

20. After a few minutes, Kelly decides not to watch the movie. Sanja is _____ in the

    line now.

21. Ben has just arrived at the theater. If he wants to watch the movie, he must stand

    after _____.

Color the correct answer in each set of pictures.

22. The 3rd duck from the left

23. The 10th dolphin from the right

24. The 5th strawberry from the left

25. The 6th swan from the left

26. The 1st candle from the left

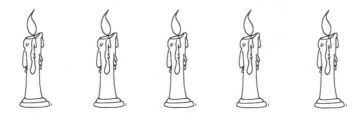

Singapore Math Level 1A & 1B

27. The 4th watch from the left

28. The eighth bag from the right

29. The 3rd key from the right

30. The first lamp from the left

31. The 5th strawberry from the right

32. Draw a hat on the second girl from the left

79

Singapore Math Level 1A & 1B

33. Use the clues below to help you solve the riddle.

Clues:

| T G O N H U D |

(a) 7th letter from the left

(b) 5th letter from the right

(c) 6th letter from the left

(d) 2nd letter from the left

(e) 5th letter from the left

(f) 4th letter from the right

(g) 2nd letter from the right

(h) 1st letter from the left

What kind of nut has a hole in it?

___ ___ ___ ___ ___ ___ ___ ___
(a)   (b)   (c)   (d)   (e)   (f)   (g)   (h)

Singapore Math Level 1A & 1B

1. Circle the 2nd hen.

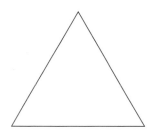

1st

Identify each shape by filling in the correct letters.

2.

t r _ _ _ g _ e

3.

r _ _ t _ n _ l e

Singapore Math Level 1A & 1B

Write the correct words or symbols on the lines provided.

4. 6th   _____

5. first   _____

6. third   _____

7. 8th   _____

Complete the patterns.

8.

9.

10.

11. Color the 1st leaf from the right.

Singapore Math Level 1A & 1B

12. Color the 3rd wheel from the left.

13. Draw a flower in the 4th vase from the left.

14. Draw an orange on the 7th plate from the right.

Circle the shape that is exactly like the one in the box.

15.

16.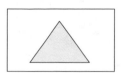

Singapore Math Level 1A & 1B

Fill in the blanks with the correct names of the children.

Rachel   Alyssa   Maddy   Carmen

17. _____ is standing 1st from the right.

18. _____ is standing between Rachel and Maddy.

19. _____ is standing next to Carmen.

20. Maddy is standing between _____ and Carmen.

Singapore Math Level 1A & 1B

Unit 7: NUMBERS 1–20

Examples:

1. Write 20 as a word.   twenty

2. Write seventeen as a numeral.   <u>17</u>

3. 10 and 5 make ___.   10 + 5 = <u>15</u>

4. 18 = ___ ten ___ ones   <u>1</u> ten <u>8</u> ones

5. Compare the numbers below.

    <u>13</u> is the smallest number.

    <u>16</u> is between **13** and **19**.

    <u>19</u> is the largest number.

6. Complete the number pattern.

    19, 18, 17, ___, ___, ___   19, 18, 17, <u>16</u>, <u>15</u>, <u>14</u>

Count the objects in each group. Write the correct number on the line.

1.

   _____

3.

   _____

2.

   _____

4.

   _____

Count the objects in each group. Write the correct number in words on the line.

5.

   _____

7.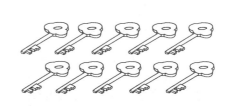

   _____

6.

   _____

8.

   _____

Singapore Math Level 1A & 1B

Write the correct numerals or words on the lines.

9. 11   _____

10. eighteen   _____

11. 20   _____

12. twelve   _____

13. 14   _____

14. 12   _____

15. thirteen   _____

16. 16   _____

17. seventeen   _____

18. 19   _____

Study the pictures below. Fill in each blank with the correct answer.

19.

10 and 6 make _____.

20.

10 and 4 make _____.

21.

10 and 8 make _____.

Singapore Math Level 1A & 1B

Fill in each blank with the correct answer.

22. 10 and 3 make _____.

23. 10 and 7 make _____.

24. 10 and 4 make _____.

25. 10 and 1 make _____.

26. 10 and 10 make _____.

27. 10 and 6 make _____.

28. 10 and 2 make _____.

29. 10 and 9 make _____.

30. 10 and 5 make _____.

31. 10 and 8 make _____.

For each set, circle a group of 10 items. Then, fill in the blanks with the correct answers.

32.

_____ ten _____ ones = _____

34.

_____ ten _____ ones = _____

33.

_____ ten _____ ones = _____

35.

_____ ten _____ ones = _____

Fill in each blank with the correct answer.

36. _____ ten and 8 ones = 18

37. _____ ten and 1 one = 11

38. 1 ten and _____ ones = 17

39. 1 ten and _____ ones = 12

40. _____ ten and _____ ones = 15

41. _____ ten and _____ ones = 19

Singapore Math Level 1A & 1B

Color the picture that shows the smaller number. Fill in each blank with the correct answer.

42.

_____ is smaller than _____.

43.

_____ is smaller than _____.

44.

_____ is smaller than _____.

Color the picture that shows the larger number. Fill in each blank with the correct answer.

45.

_____ is greater than _____.

Singapore Math Level 1A & 1B

46.

_____ is greater than _____.

47.

_____ is greater than _____.

Circle the vase that shows the smallest number.

48.

   11

49.

   18

50.

Singapore Math Level 1A & 1B

Circle the flower that shows the largest number.

51.

52.

53.

Complete the number patterns.

54. 8, 9, 10, _____, _____

55. 19, 18, _____, 16, _____

56. _____, 13, _____, 11, 10

Fill in each blank with the correct answer.

57. 1 more than 16 is _____.

58. 3 more than 11 is _____.

59. _____ is 2 less than 13.

60. _____ is 3 less than 19.

61. _____ is 4 less than 20.

Singapore Math Level 1A & 1B

62. Arrange the following numbers from the largest to the smallest.

    16   18   11   20   15

    _____   _____   _____   _____   _____
    largest

63. Arrange the following numbers from the largest to the smallest.

    11   19   10   17   13

    _____   _____   _____   _____   _____
    largest

64. Arrange the following numbers from the smallest to the largest.

    19   20   14   18   16

    _____   _____   _____   _____   _____
    smallest

65. Arrange the following numbers from the smallest to the largest.

    13   10   14   17   12

    _____   _____   _____   _____   _____
    smallest

Singapore Math Level 1A & 1B

Unit 8: ADDING AND SUBTRACTING NUMBERS UP TO 20

Examples:

1. $6 + 9 = 10 + 5$

    $= \underline{\mathbf{15}}$

    1   5

2. $15 + 2 = 5 + 2 = 7$

    $= 7 + 10$

    $= \underline{\mathbf{17}}$

    10   5

3. $17 - 6 = 7 - 6 = 1$

    $= 10 + 1$

    $= \underline{\mathbf{11}}$

    10   7

4. $11 - 8 = 10 - 8 = 2$

    $= 2 + 1$

    $= \underline{\mathbf{3}}$

    1   10

Singapore Math Level 1A & 1B

Complete each addition sentence.

1.

5 + ____ = ____

2.

12 + ____ = ____

3.

10 + ____ = ____

4.

8 + ____ = ____

Solve the problems below by grouping the items into 10s.

5.

6 + 7 = ____

6.

8 + 3 = ____

7.

8 + 7 = ____

8.

12 + 8 = ____

Singapore Math Level 1A & 1B

Solve each addition problem by first making a 10.

Example:

9 + 4 = **13**

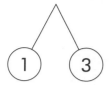

9 + 1 = 10

10 + 3 = 3

9.   6 + 5 = ____

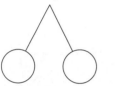

___ + ___ = ___

___ + ___ = ___

10.   7 + 7 = ____

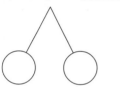

___ + ___ = ___

___ + ___ = ___

11.   7 + 8 = ____

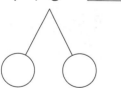

___ + ___ = ___

___ + ___ = ___

12.   9 + 9 = ____

___ + ___ = ___

___ + ___ = ___

Singapore Math Level 1A & 1B

Fill in each blank with the correct answer.

13.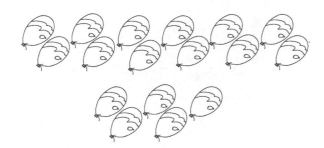

$12 + 5 =$ ____

14.

$9 + 4 =$ ____

15.

$11 + 4 =$ ____

16.

$7 + 8 =$ ____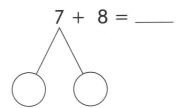

17.

$5 + 12 =$ ____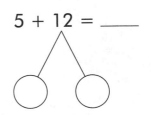

96

Complete each subtraction sentence.

18.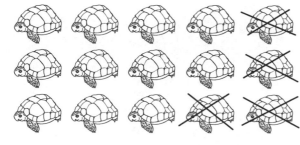

    _____ – 4 = _____

20.

    18 – _____ = _____

19.

    _____ – 5 = _____

21.

    _____ – 3 = _____

Solve each subtraction problem by first making a 10.

Example:

13 – 3 = **10**

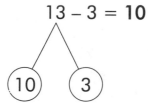

3 – 3 = 0

10 + 0 = 10

22.   18 – 6 = _____

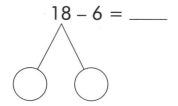

_____ – _____ = _____

_____ + _____ = _____

Singapore Math Level 1A & 1B

23. $17 - 4 =$ _____   _____ $-$ _____ $=$ _____

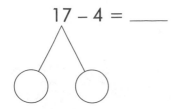

                                                 _____ $+$ _____ $=$ _____

24. $15 - 4 =$ _____   _____ $-$ _____ $=$ _____

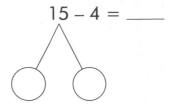

                                                 _____ $+$ _____ $=$ _____

25. $14 - 4 =$ _____   _____ $-$ _____ $=$ _____

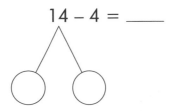

                                                 _____ $+$ _____ $=$ _____

Fill in each blank with the correct answer.

26.
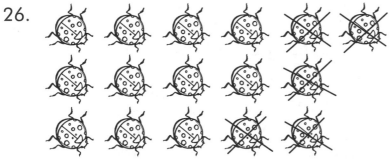
                        $16 - 5 =$ _____

27.
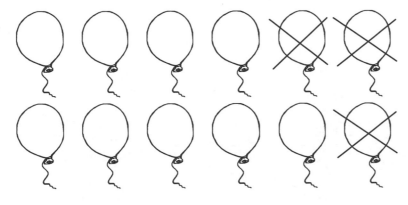
                        $12 - 3 =$ _____

Singapore Math Level 1A & 1B

28. 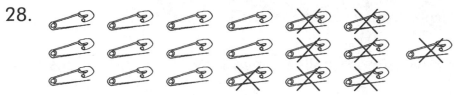 $19 - 8 =$ ____
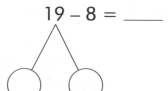

29. 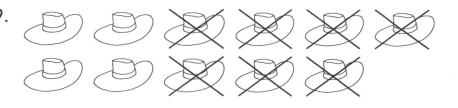 $11 - 7 =$ ____

30. 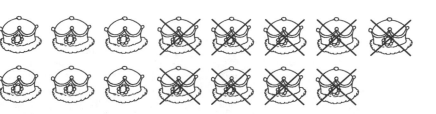 $15 - 9 =$ ____
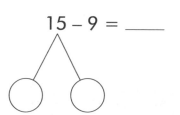

Fill in each blank with the correct answer.

31. $17 - 9 =$ ____

32. $20 - 3 =$ ____

33. $6 + 7 =$ ____

34. ____ $+ 8 = 11$

35. ____ $- 4 = 9$

36. $12 -$ ____ $= 7$

37. $16 +$ ____ $= 16$

38. $9 +$ ____ $= 18$

39. $15 -$ ____ $= 9$

40. $13 +$ ____ $= 18$

Write + or − in each circle to solve the problem.

41. $6 \bigcirc 7 = 13$

42. $15 \bigcirc 8 = 7$

43. $17 \bigcirc 2 = 19$

44. $11 \bigcirc 5 = 6$

45. $8 \bigcirc 9 = 17$

Solve each story problem. Show your work in the space below.

46. Eliza has 8 dolls. Her sister buys 6 more dolls for her. How many dolls does Eliza have altogether?

Eliza has _____ dolls altogether.

47. Imani has 18 stickers. She gives 9 stickers to Aiden. How many stickers does Imani have now?

Imani has _____ stickers now.

Singapore Math Level 1A & 1B

48. Mike colors 6 stars blue. He colors another 7 stars red. How many stars does Mike color altogether?

Mike colors _____ stars altogether.

49. Sarah bought 4 flowers on Monday. She bought another 10 flowers on Tuesday. How many flowers did Sarah buy in 2 days?

Sarah bought _____ flowers in 2 days.

50. Peter has 15 toy cars. Sam has 8 toy cars. How many more toy cars does Peter have than Sam?

Peter has _____ more toy cars than Sam.

Singapore Math Level 1A & 1B

Unit 9: LENGTH

Examples:

Look at the picture below. Use it to answer the questions that follow.

A ●————————————●

B ●————————————●

C ●————————●

1. Which line is the longest?   **B**

2. Which line is the shortest?   **C**

3. Line **A** is shorter than line **B** but longer than line **C**.

Each 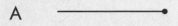 stands for 1 unit.

4. How long is the length of the folder?   **15 units**

102

Singapore Math Level 1A & 1B

Circle the correct answer.

1. Which ribbon is shorter?

2. Who is taller?

3. Which teapot is higher?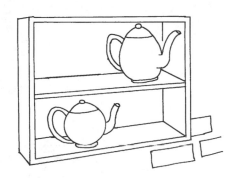

4. Draw a line shorter than Line A.

   Line A _____

5. Draw a stick longer than Stick A.

   Stick A

Singapore Math Level 1A & 1B

6. Draw a ruler longer than Ruler A.

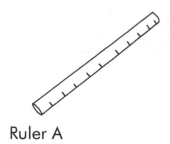

Ruler A

7. Draw a kite flying higher than Kite A.

Kite A

8. Color the tallest building.

9. Color the shortest pencil.

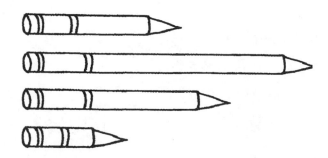

Fill in the blanks with the words taller, tallest, shorter, **and** shortest.

10. Amelia is the _____ girl.

11. Lily is _____ than Mira but _____ than Amelia.

12. Lauren is the _____ girl.

Fill in the blanks with higher **or** highest.

13. Takashi is standing on the _____ level.

14. Zachary is standing on a _____ level than Jonah.

Singapore Math Level 1A & 1B

Count the units. Fill in each blank with the correct answer.

15.

    The frog is _____ long.

16.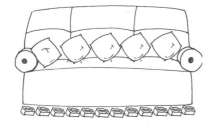

    The microwave oven is _____

    _____ long and _____ _____ tall.

17.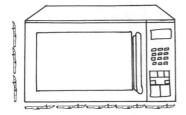

    The sofa is as long as _____ 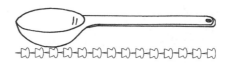.

18. Each _____ stands for 1 unit.

    The file is _____ units long.

19. Each _____ stands for 1 unit.

    The ladle is _____ units long.

Singapore Math Level 1A & 1B

Each ☐ **stands for 1 unit. Fill in each blank with the correct answer.**

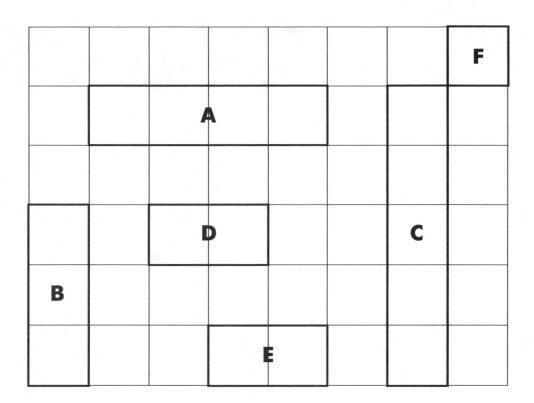

20. Strip _____ is the longest.

    It is _____ units long.

21. Strip _____ is the shortest.

    It is _____ unit long.

22. Strip _____ is as long as Strip _____.

23. Color the strip that is 4 units long.

REVIEW 4

Write the correct number on each line.

1.

_____

2.

_____

3.   Study the lines below. Answer the questions that follow.

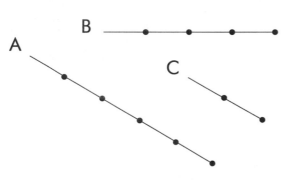

(a)   Line A is _____ units long.

(b)   Line B is _____ units long.

(c)   Line C is _____ units long.

(d)   Line D is _____ units long.

(e)   Line _____ is the longest.

(f)   Line _____ is the shortest.

(g)   Line B is longer than Line _____ by 2 units.

Fill in the missing numbers.

4.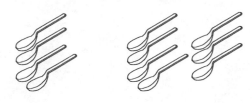

4 + ___ = ___

6.

___ – 6 = ___

5.

18 – ___ = ___

7.

___ + 9 = ___

8. Circle the smaller number.

14   17

9. Cross out the larger number.

11   13

Complete the number patterns.

10. 13, 14, ___, 16, ___

11. 19, 18, ___, ___, 15, 14

12. Arrange the following numbers from the largest to the smallest.

11   20   15   18   14

___   ___   ___   ___   ___

largest

13. Arrange the following numbers from the smallest to the largest.

11   19   16   13   17

___   ___   ___   ___   ___

smallest

Singapore Math Level 1A & 1B

Fill in each blank with the correct answer.

14. 14 = _____ ten _____ ones

15. 1 ten 6 ones = _____

16. 20 = _____ tens _____ ones

Solve each story problem. Show your work in the space below.

17. Ari has 16 markers. Sam has 5 markers fewer than Ari. How many markers does Sam have?

Sam has _____ markers.

18. Jack pays $12 for his toy robot. Natalie pays $8 more for her toy. How much does Natalie pay for her toy?

Natalie pays $_____ for her toy.

19. Alejandro saved $10 in January. He saved $18 in February. How much more did he save in February?

He saved $_____ more in February.

20. Sydney keeps 13 guppies in her tank. Amina has 5 guppies fewer than Sydney. How many guppies does Amina have?

Amina has _____ guppies.

Singapore Math Level 1A & 1B

MID-REVIEW

Count the frogs. Write the number on the line.

1.

   _____

Write the number in words on the line.

2. 17 _____

Look at the pictures carefully. Fill in each blank with the correct answer.

3.

   ____ + ____ = ____

Singapore Math Level 1A & 1B

4.

 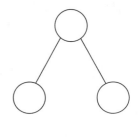

_____ – _____ = _____

5. Color the 8th insect.

1st

6. Draw a star above the 3rd girl from the left.

Fill in each blank with the correct answer.

7. _____ – 5 = 15

8. _____ + 7 = 12

9. 3 + _____ = 9

10. 16 – _____ = 12

11. 11 – _____ = 0

Singapore Math Level 1A & 1B

Fill in the missing numbers on the lines.

12. 4, _____, 6, _____, 8, 9, 10

Name the shapes.

13.

14.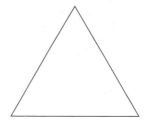

_____   _____

Write the correct ordinal number or symbol on the lines.

15. second   _____

16. 10th   _____

Fill in each blank with the correct answer.

17. 2 tens = _____

18. 13 = _____ ten _____ ones

19. Circle the object that is exactly the same as the one in the box.

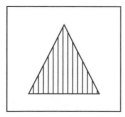   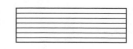

Singapore Math Level 1A & 1B

20.

(a) _____ is the longest.

(b) E is longer than _____.

(c) D is _____ units long.

(d) C is _____ units longer than B.

(e) Add _____ units to E to make it as long as A.

Solve the story problems. Show your work in the space below.

21. Suzanna has 13 apples. She gives 6 apples to her friends. How many apples does she have left?

She has _____ apples left.

22. Marcos saves $8 in March and $11 in April.

   (a)   How much does he save altogether?

He saves $_____ altogether.

Singapore Math Level 1A & 1B

(b) How much more does he save in April than in March?

He saves $_____ more in April than in March.

23. Thomas has collected 7 toy planes. He wants to have a collection of 20 toy planes. How many more toy planes does he need to collect?

He needs to collect _____ more toy planes.

24. A doll costs $15. Bailey has only $9 now. How much more money does she need in order to buy the doll?

She needs $_____ more.

25. Alicia made 12 bookmarks for her friends. She made 4 bookmarks for her teachers. How many bookmarks did she make altogether?

She made _____ bookmarks altogether.

Singapore Math Level 1A & 1B

CHALLENGE QUESTIONS

Read each of the following questions carefully. Fill in the blanks with your answers.

1. Fill in the blanks with numbers from 1 to 5 so that the sum of the 3 circles along each line is 10. Use each number only ONCE.

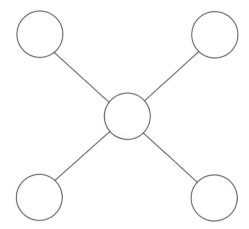

2. Six students were sitting in a school auditorium. They were seated facing the stage.

    • Cameron sat next to Sean.
    • Jonathan sat next to Sean.
    • Rosa sat farther away from the stage.
    • Antwon sat behind Jonathan.
    • Cameron sat in front of Kayla.

    Fill in each box with the correct name.

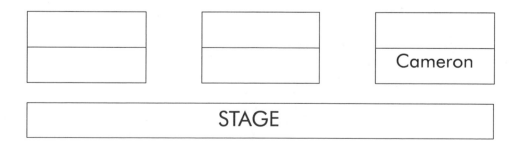

3. Mei has a ruler.
   Nicholas's ruler is longer than Mei's.
   Ivana has a ruler longer than Mei's but shorter than Nicholas's.
   Simon's ruler is shorter than Mei's.
   Who has the longest ruler?

   _____ has the longest ruler.

4. A group of boys went to the movies. They sat in the first row. Rashid, one of the boys, was seated 4th from the left and 3rd from the right. How many boys went to the movies?

   _____ boys went to the movies.

5. Fill in each circle with numbers from 1 to 9 to make the addition sentence true. Use each number only ONCE.

$$\bigcirc + \bigcirc + \bigcirc = 17$$

6. Find the mystery 2-digit number based on these hints.

   • The first digit is smaller than 3.
   • The first digit is an odd number.
   • The second digit is an even number.
   • The difference between the first digit and the second digit is 5.

   The 2-digit number is _____.

Singapore Math Level 1A & 1B

7. How many routes can the mouse take in order to get the cheese? The mouse must travel along the dotted lines within the shortest time.

The mouse can take _____ routes in order to get the cheese.

8. Study the patterns below and draw the correct shape in each box.

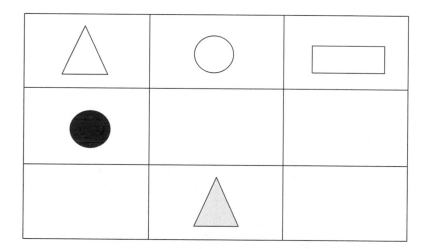

9. 9 students are standing in line at a drinking fountain during recess. Joel comes along and joins the line. There are 6 students between Joel and Mia. In which position is Mia from the fountain?

Mia is _____ from the drinking fountain.

Singapore Math Level 1A & 1B

10. Fill in each shaded box with numbers from 0 to 9. The numbers in the 3 boxes along each side should add up to 10. Use each number only ONCE. Which numbers are not used?

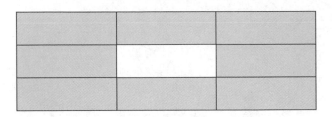

Numbers _____ and _____ are not used.

11. I am a 2-digit number. My 2 digits and the sum of my 2 digits are in sequence. What number am I?

I am _____.

12. How many triangles can be formed from the shape below? The triangles must be of the same size.

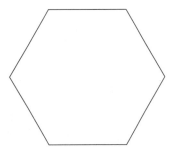

_____ triangles can be formed from the shape.

Singapore Math Level 1A & 1B

1B LEARNING OUTCOMES

Unit 10 Mass
Students should be able to
- find the mass of objects in units.
- compare and arrange the mass of objects.
- understand the words *light*, *lighter*, *lightest*, *heavy*, *heavier*, and *heaviest*.

Unit 11 Picture Graphs
Students should be able to
- create picture graphs based on the given data.
- understand and interpret data from picture graphs.

Review 5
This review tests students' understanding of Units 10 & 11.

Unit 12 Numbers 1-40
Students should be able to
- recognize numbers up to 40.
- group numbers into tens and ones.
- compare numbers up to 40.
- arrange numbers in order up to 40.
- complete number patterns.
- add and subtract numbers up to 40.
- add 3 numbers.
- solve addition and subtraction story problems.

Unit 13 Mental Calculations
Students should be able to
- add 2 numbers without regrouping mentally.
- subtract 2 numbers without regrouping mentally.

Unit 14 Multiplying
Students should be able to
- write correct multiplication sentences.
- find the total in multiplication sentences.
- solve 1-step multiplication story problems.

Review 6
This review tests students' understanding of Units 12, 13, & 14.

Unit 15 Dividing
Students should be able to
- find the number of items in each group.
- find the number of groups.

Unit 16 Time
Students should be able to
- read time at the hour and half hour.

Review 7
This review tests students' understanding of Units 15 & 16.

Unit 17 Numbers 1-100
Students should be able to
- recognize numbers up to 100.
- group numbers into tens and ones.
- compare numbers up to 100.
- complete number patterns.
- add and subtract numbers up to 100.
- solve 1-step story problems.

Unit 18 Money (Part 1)
Students should be able to
- count coins and bills in different denominations.
- match money of one denomination to the same value of another denomination.

Unit 19 Money (Part 2)
Students should be able to
- perform addition and subtraction in dollars.
- perform addition and subtraction in cents.
- solve story problems related to money.

Review 8
This review tests students' understanding of Units 17, 18, & 19.

Final Review
This review is an excellent assessment of students' understanding of all the topics in the second half this book.

Singapore Math Level 1A & 1B

FORMULA SHEET

Unit 10 Mass

Comparing the mass of 2 objects

When 2 objects of different masses are placed on a balance, the object that sinks is heavier.

When 2 objects of different masses are placed on a balance, the object that rises is lighter.

When both sides of the balance are equal in height, the objects have the same mass.

To find the mass of an object, look at the number of units needed to balance the mass of the object.

Unit 11 Picture Graphs

To create a picture graph,
- collect data.
- organize and place the data in a table.

You can read and use the picture graph to answer questions.

Note that the symbol used in the picture graph stands for 1 item.

Unit 12 Numbers 1-40

Numerals	Words	Numerals	Words
21	twenty-one	31	thirty-one
22	twenty-two	32	thirty-two
23	twenty-three	33	thirty-three
24	twenty-four	34	thirty-four
25	twenty-five	35	thirty-five
26	twenty-six	36	thirty-six
27	twenty-seven	37	thirty-seven
28	twenty-eight	38	thirty-eight
29	twenty-nine	39	thirty-nine
30	thirty	40	forty

Place value

Numbers greater than 10 can be grouped into tens and ones.

Example:

35 = **3** tens **5** ones

Number patterns

When completing number patterns,
- see if the number pattern is in an increasing or a decreasing order.
- observe the difference between each number.
- add or subtract to get the next number.

Number order

When arranging numbers in order, determine if the series starts with the smallest or the largest number.

Comparing numbers

The words *greater than* and *more than* mean addition (+).

The words *smaller than* and *less than* mean subtraction (–).

The word *is* means equal to (=).

Example:

_____ is 3 more than 19.

_____ = 3 + 19

Adding numbers

- Add the digits in the ones place first.
- If the answer is more than 9, regroup the ones and carry a one to the tens place.
- Add the digits in the tens place. Remember to add the one that was carried if there is one.

Subtracting numbers

- Subtract the digits in the ones place first.
- If subtraction is not possible in the ones place, regroup the tens and lend a ten (10) to the ones.
- Subtract the digits in the ones place.
- Then, subtract the digits in the tens place.

Adding 3 numbers

- Make a ten first.
- Add the remaining numbers to get a sum.
- Add the ten to the sum to get the final answer.

Unit 13 Mental Calculations

Adding a 2-digit number and a 1-digit number mentally

Singapore Math Level 1A & 1B

- Regroup the 2-digit number into tens and ones.
- Add the ones to get a sum.
- Add the sum to the tens to get the final answer.

Adding a 2-digit number and tens mentally
- Regroup the 2-digit number into tens and ones.
- Add the tens to get a sum.
- Add the ones to the sum to get the final answer.

Subtracting a 1-digit number from a 2-digit number mentally
- Regroup the 2-digit number into tens and ones.
- Subtract the ones.
- Add the ones to the tens to get the final answer.

Subtracting tens from a 2-digit number mentally
- Regroup the 2-digit number into tens and ones.
- Subtract the tens to get the result.
- Add the result to the ones to get the final answer.

Unit 14 Multiplication

Multiplication is repeated addition.

The sign $\times$ is used to represent multiplication in a number sentence.

Example:

$$4 + 4 + 4 = 12$$
$$3 \times 4 = 12$$

Unit 15 Division

Division is the opposite of multiplication.

Division allows us to find the equal number of items in each group. It also allows us to find the number of groups.

Unit 16 Time

There are 2 hands on the face of a clock.
The short hand is called the *hour hand*. The long hand is called the *minute hand*.

Numbers 1 to 12 are displayed on the face of the clock. There are 24 hours in a day, so the hour and minute hands go around twice every day.

When the hour hand is at 2 and the minute hand is at 12, the time is read as 2 o'clock.

When the hour hand is between 2 and 3 and the minute hand is at 6, the time is read as 2:30.

Unit 17 Numbers 1-100

Numerals	Words
50	fifty
60	sixty
70	seventy
80	eighty
90	ninety
100	one hundred

Adding a 2-digit number and a 2-digit number
- Add the digits in the ones place. If the sum is more than 10, regroup the ones and carry a one to the tens place.
- Add the digits in the tens place. Add the one that was carried if there is one.

Subtracting a 2-digit number from a 2-digit number
- Subtract the digits in the ones place. If it is not possible, regroup the tens and lend a ten (10) to the ones.
- Subtract the digits in the tens place accordingly.

Unit 18 Money (Part 1)
The symbol for cents is ¢.
The symbol for dollars is $.

Ways of exchanging coins
1 ten-cent coin = 2 five-cent coins
1 twenty-five cent coin = 5 five-cent coins
                       = 25 one-cent coins
1 fifty-cent coin = 5 ten-cent coins
1 dollar coin = 10 ten-cent coins
             = 4 twenty-five-cent coins
             = 2 fifty-cent coins

Ways of exchanging bills
1 one-dollar bill = 1 one-dollar coin
1 ten-dollar bill = 10 one-dollar coins
                 = 2 five-dollar bills

Unit 19 Money (Part 2)
Adding in cents or in dollars
1. Add the digits in the ones place. If the sum is more than 10, carry a one to the tens place.
2. Add the digits in the tens place. Add the one that was carried if there is one.

Subtracting in cents or in dollars
1. Subtract the digits in the ones place. If this is not possible, lend a ten (10) to the ones.
2. Subtract the digits in the tens place.

Singapore Math Level 1A & 1B

Unit 10: MASS

Examples:

1. Which of the following fruits is heavier?

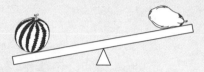

The **watermelon** is heavier than the papaya.

2. Study the pictures, and fill in each blank with the correct answer.
    Each ⬦ stands for 1 unit.

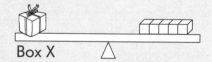   

(a) Box **Y** is heavier than Box **X**.

(b) Box **X** is lighter than Box **Y**.

3. Study the pictures carefully, and fill in each blank with the correct answer.

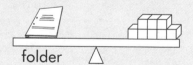   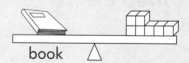   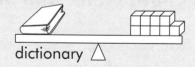

(a) The mass of the folder is about **8** units.

(b) The mass of the book is about **7** units.

(c) The mass of the dictionary is about **9** units.

(d) Arrange these items in order. Begin with the lightest.
     book, folder, dictionary

Fill in each blank with as heavy as, heavier than, **or** lighter than.

1.

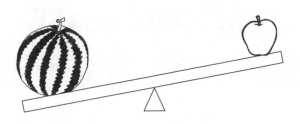

The apple is _____ the watermelon.

2.

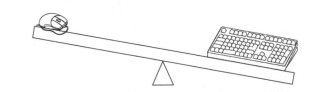

The keyboard is _____ the computer mouse.

3.

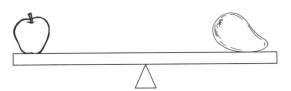

The apple is _____ the mango.

Fill in each blank with the correct answer.

4. Each ⬤ stands for 1 unit.

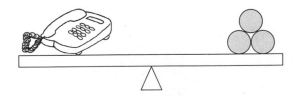

The mass of the telephone is _____ units.

Singapore Math Level 1A & 1B

5. Each ▢ stands for 1 unit.

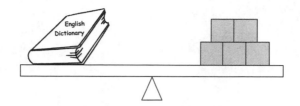

The mass of the dictionary is _____ units.

6. Each ✏ stands for 1 unit.

The mass of the schoolbag is _____ units.

7. Each ⬚ stands for 1 unit.

The mass of the water bottle is _____ units.

Singapore Math Level 1A & 1B

Fill in each blank with the correct answer.

Each ⬤ stands for 1 unit.

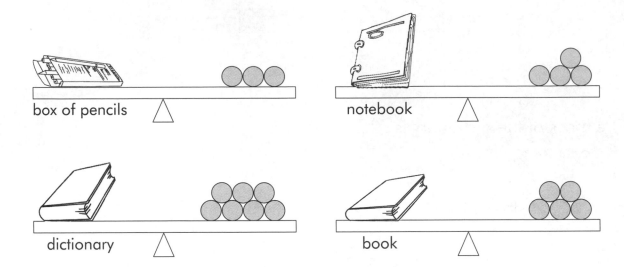

8. The mass of the notebook is _____ units.

9. The mass of the dictionary is _____ units.

10. The mass of the box of pencils is _____ units.

11. The mass of the book is _____ units.

12. The _____ is heavier than the book.

13. The _____ is lighter than the notebook.

14. The _____ is the heaviest.

15. The _____ is the lightest.

16. Arrange the 4 items in order. Begin with the lightest.

_____, _____, _____, _____
   lightest

Singapore Math Level 1A & 1B

Fill in each blank with the correct answer.

Each ⬤ stands for 1 unit.

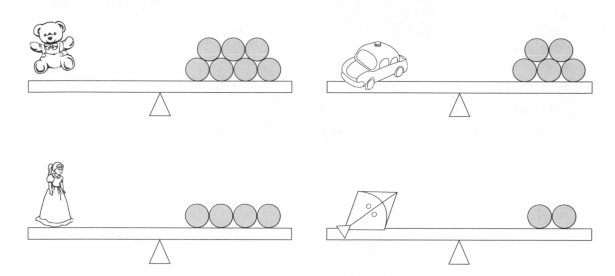

17. The mass of the teddy bear is _____ units.

18. The mass of the toy car is _____ units.

19. The mass of the doll is _____ units.

20. The mass of the kite is _____ units.

21. The doll is heavier than the _____.

22. The toy car is lighter than the _____.

23. The _____ is the lightest.

24. The _____ is the heaviest.

25. The _____ is lighter than the toy car but heavier than the kite.

Singapore Math Level 1A & 1B

Fill in each blank with the correct answer.

Each 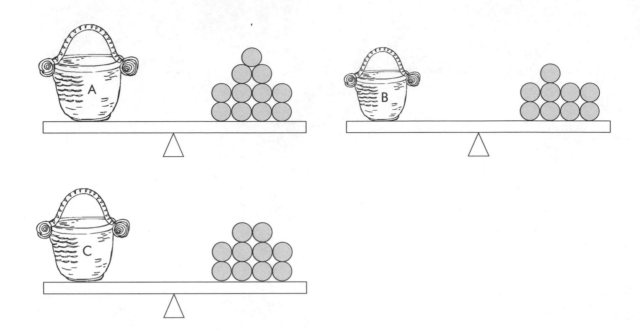 stands for 1 unit.

26. The mass of Basket A is _____ units.

27. The mass of Basket B is _____ units.

28. The mass of Basket C is _____ units.

29. Basket _____ is lighter than Basket C.

30. Basket _____ is heavier than Basket C.

31. Basket _____ is the heaviest.

32. Basket _____ is the lightest.

33. Arrange the baskets in order. Begin with the heaviest.

_____, _____, _____
   heaviest

Singapore Math Level 1A & 1B

Fill in each blank with the correct answer.

Each ◯ stands for 1 unit.

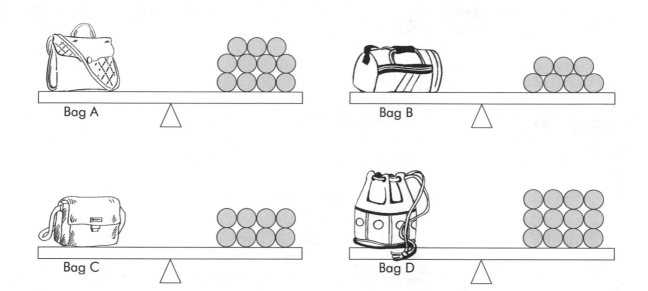

34. Bag _____ is the heaviest.

35. Bag _____ is the lightest.

36. The mass of Bag A is _____ units.

37. The mass of Bag D is _____ units.

38. Bag C is heavier than Bag _____.

39. Bag _____ is heavier than Bag C but lighter than Bag D.

40. Arrange the 4 bags in order. Begin with the heaviest.

_____, _____, _____, _____
  heaviest

Unit 11: PICTURE GRAPHS

Examples:

This graph shows the number of stickers collected by a group of children in a week.

Sam	◯ ◯ ◯ ◯ ◯ ◯ ◯
Eduardo	◯ ◯ ◯ ◯ ◯ ◯
Nick	◯ ◯ ◯ ◯
Kelly	◯ ◯ ◯ ◯ ◯ ◯ ◯ ◯ ◯

Each ◯ stands for 1 sticker.

(a)   How many stickers did Eduardo collect?   <u>6</u>

(b)   How many stickers did Kelly collect?   <u>9</u>

(c)   How many more stickers did Eduardo collect than Nick?   <u>2</u>

(d)   How many fewer stickers did Nick collect than Kelly?   <u>5</u>

(e)   Who collected the most stickers?   <u>Kelly</u>

(f)   Who collected the fewest stickers?   <u>Nick</u>

(g)   How many stickers did the children collect in a week?

7 + 6 + 4 + 9 = <u>26</u>

1. Anna went to the zoo last Sunday. Study the picture carefully. Draw a picture graph of the animals she saw in the zoo. Use ● to stand for 1 animal.

Monkeys	
Lions	
Tigers	
Giraffes	
Parrots	

Singapore Math Level 1A & 1B

2. Study the picture carefully. Draw a picture graph of the games the children are playing. Use ⭐ to stand for 1 child.

Hopscotch	Soccer	Jumping Rope	Marbles

Singapore Math Level 1A & 1B

3. The picture below shows a group of children at the park. Study the picture carefully. Draw a picture graph of the activities the children are doing. Use  to stand for 1 child.

Soccer	
Kite-Flying	
Feeding Ducks	
Walking	

Singapore Math Level 1A & 1B

The graph below shows food Mrs. Lee sells at her restaurant. Study the graph carefully. Fill in each blank with the correct answer.

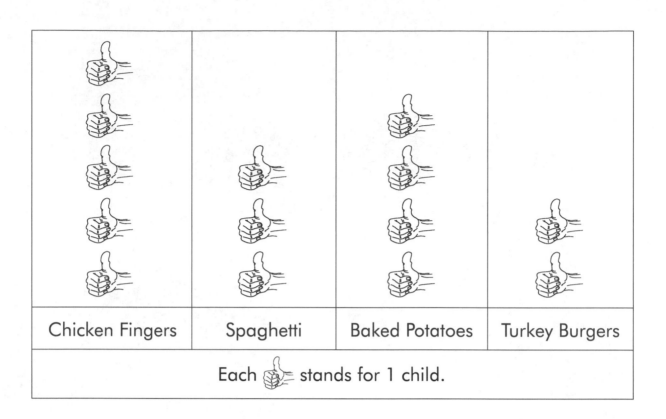

4. _____ children buy baked potatoes.

5. _____ children buy chicken fingers.

6. The least popular food is the _____.

7. The most popular food is the _____.

8. _____ more children buy baked potatoes than turkey burgers.

9. _____ fewer children buy spaghetti than chicken fingers.

This graph shows the favorite sports of the students in a class. Study the graph carefully. Fill in each blank with the correct answer.

Basketball	
Swimming	
Football	
Baseball	
Karate	

Each stands for 1 student.

10. _____ students like baseball.

11. _____ students like football.

12. The most popular sport is _____.

13. The least popular sport is _____.

14. The number of students who like _____ and

_____ is the same.

15. _____ more students like basketball than karate.

16. _____ fewer students like karate than football.

17. There are _____ students in the class altogether.

Singapore Math Level 1A & 1B

The graph below shows the types of insects in a school garden. Study the graph carefully. Fill in each blank with the correct answer.

Butterflies	Bees	Ants	Ladybugs
🌳🌳🌳🌳	🌳🌳🌳🌳🌳	🌳🌳🌳🌳🌳🌳🌳	🌳🌳

Each 🌳 stands for 1 insect.

18. There are _____ butterflies.

19. There are _____ ladybugs.

20. There are more _____ than other insects.

21. There are fewer _____ than other insects.

22. There are _____ fewer butterflies than ants.

23. There are _____ more bees than ladybugs.

24. There are _____ insects altogether.

REVIEW 5

The picture graph below shows the number of cups of water each container can hold. Study the graph carefully. Fill in each blank with the correct answer.

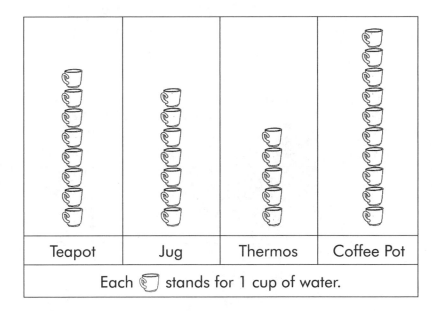

1. The teapot can hold _____ cups of water.

2. The thermos can hold _____ cups of water.

3. The container that can hold the fewest cups of water is the _____.

4. The container that can hold the most cups of water is the _____.

5. The teapot can hold _____ more cups of water than the thermos.

6. The jug can hold _____ fewer cups of water than the coffee pot.

Singapore Math Level 1A & 1B

Fill in each blank with the correct answer.

Each 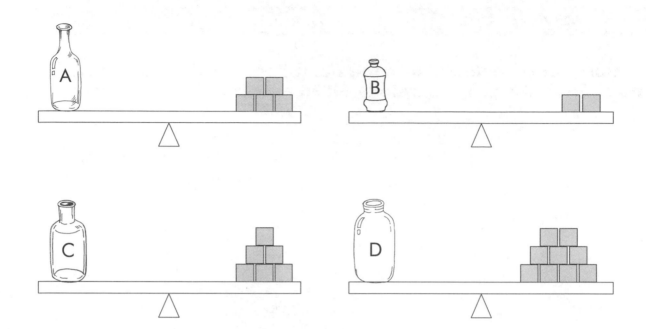 stands for 1 unit.

7.   The mass of Bottle A is _____ units.

8.   The mass of Bottle B is _____ units.

9.   The mass of Bottle C is _____ units.

10. The mass of Bottle D is _____ units.

11. Bottle _____ is the heaviest.

12. Bottle _____ is the lightest.

Singapore Math Level 1A & 1B

13. The picture below shows a class of students at a park. Study the picture carefully. Draw a picture graph of the activities the students are doing.

Kite-Flying	Riding Bikes	Feeding Birds	Walking
Each ⭐ stands for 1 student.			

Singapore Math Level 1A & 1B

Fill in each blank with heavier than, lighter than, **or** as heavy as.

14.

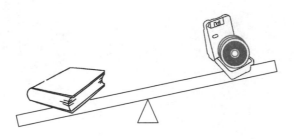

The book is _____ the CDs.

15.

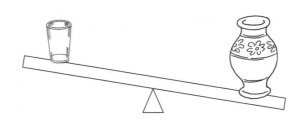

The glass is _____ the vase.

16.

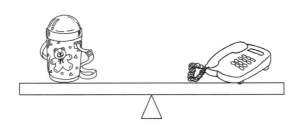

The water bottle is _____ the telephone.

17.

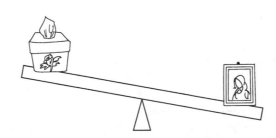

The picture frame is _____ the box of tissues.

Singapore Math Level 1A & 1B

Fill in each blank with the correct answer. Each ▢ stands for 1 unit.

18.

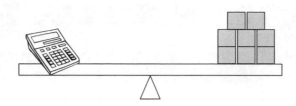

The mass of the calculator is _____ units.

19.

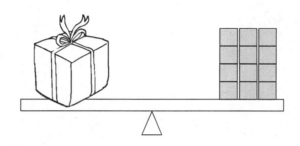

The mass of the present is _____ units.

20.

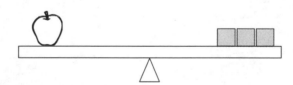

The mass of the apple is _____ units.

Singapore Math Level 1A & 1B

Unit 12 : NUMBERS 1-40

Examples:

1. 5 and 20 make **25**.

2. **38** is 2 less than 40.

3. $29 + 2 = $ **31**

	Tens	Ones
	^{1}2	9
+		2
	3	1

4. $38 - 19 = $ **19**

	Tens	Ones
	^{2}3̸	^{18}8̸
−	1	9
	1	9

Circle groups of 10 in each set of pictures. Count the items, and write the correct answers on the lines.

1.

_____

2.

_____

3.

_____

4.

_____

5.

_____

Singapore Math Level 1A & 1B

6. Write the following numbers in words.

   (a) 20 _____

   (b) 15 _____

   (c) 39 _____

   (d) 27 _____

   (e) 11 _____

   (f) 40 _____

   (g) 35 _____

   (h) 21 _____

7. Write the correct numbers on the lines provided.

   (a) fourteen _____   (e) twenty-six _____

   (b) twenty-four _____   (f) eighteen _____

   (c) thirty _____   (g) thirty-two _____

   (d) nineteen _____   (h) thirteen _____

8. Fill in each blank with the correct answer.

   (a) 30 and 6 make _____.   (e) 30 and 3 make _____.

   (b) 20 and 1 make _____.   (f) 10 and 4 make _____.

   (c) 10 and 7 make _____.   (g) 20 and 6 make _____.

   (d) 20 and 8 make _____.   (h) 30 and 9 make _____.

Fill in each blank with the correct answer.

9.

    _____ tens _____ ones = _____

12.

    _____ tens _____ ones = _____

10.

    _____ tens _____ ones = _____

13.

    _____ ten _____ ones = _____

11.

    _____ tens _____ ones = _____

14.

    _____ tens _____ ones = _____

Fill in each blank with the correct answer.

15.

    2 more than 16 is _____.

16.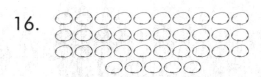

    5 less than 35 is _____.

17. 3 more than 24 is _____.

18. 1 more than 39 is _____.

19. 9 less than 28 is _____.

Singapore Math Level 1A & 1B

20.

| 35 | 22 | 28 | 17 |

(a)   The largest number is _____.

(b)   The smallest number is _____.

(c)   _____ is greater than 28.

(d)   _____ is smaller than 22.

(e)   28 is greater than _____ and _____ but smaller than _____.

21.

| 16 | 31 | 40 | 27 |

(a)   The smallest number is _____.

(b)   The largest number is _____.

(c)   2 more than 29 is _____.

(d)   2 less than 29 is _____.

(e)   _____ and _____ are smaller than 40 but greater than 16.

22.

| 19 | 40 | 21 | 35 |

(a)   The largest number is _____.

(b)   The smallest number is _____.

(c)   _____ is 2 more than 19.

(d)   _____ is 5 less than 40.

(e)   _____ is smaller than 35 but greater than 19.

23.

| 28 | 14 | 17 | 31 | 25 |

(a) The smallest number is _____.

(b) The largest number is _____.

(c) _____ is 3 more than 28.

(d) _____ is 3 less than 17.

(e) _____ is greater than 17 but smaller than 28.

Match the problems on the left to the answers on the right.

24. 2 less than 21   •   •   38

25. 1 more than 37   •   •   24

26. 3 more than 20   •   •   19

27. 2 more than 23   •   •   15

28. 3 less than 18   •   •   23

29. 1 less than 25   •   •   25

Complete the number patterns.

30. _____, 14, _____, 20, 23

31. 9, 14, 19, _____, _____

32. 25, _____, 35, _____, 45

33. 28, _____, 32, 34, _____

34. 18, 24, 30, _____, _____

Singapore Math Level 1A & 1B

Study the pictures below. Fill in each blank with the correct answer.

35.

    20 + 9 = _____

38.

    30 + 7 = _____

36.

    10 + 3 = _____

39.

    30 + 4 = _____

37.

    20 + 4 = _____

40. Solve the addition problems below by grouping tens and ones.

    (a) 34 + 2 = _____ tens _____ ones + _____ ones

         = _____ tens _____ ones

         = _____

    (b) 16 + 4 = _____ ten _____ ones + _____ ones

         = _____ ten _____ ones

         = _____

    (c) 22 + 7 = _____ tens _____ ones + _____ ones

         = _____ tens _____ ones

         = _____

Singapore Math Level 1A & 1B

(d) 24 + 8 = _____ tens _____ ones + _____ ones

= _____ tens _____ ones

= _____

(e) 27 + 7 = _____ tens _____ ones + _____ ones

= _____ tens _____ ones

= _____

41. Solve each addition problem below.

(a)   13
    + 13

(d)   11
    + 26

(b)   24
    + 15

(e)   30
    + 6

(c)   35
    + 2

42. Add and regroup to solve the problems.

(a)   29
    + 7

(d)   19
    + 16

(b)   15
    + 18

(e)   25
    + 6

(c)   28
    + 12

43. Match each child to the correct house.

 36    24   17    33    29

10 + 7   33 + 3   21 + 8   17 + 7   29 + 4

 A    B    C    D    E

44. Fill in each blank with the correct answer.

(a)

$$27 - 3 = \underline{\hspace{2cm}}$$

(b)

$$36 - 2 = \underline{\hspace{2cm}}$$

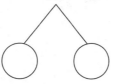

Singapore Math Level 1A & 1B

(c)

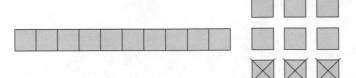

$19 - 3 = \underline{\hspace{2cm}}$

(d)

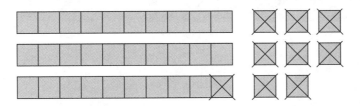

$25 - 4 = \underline{\hspace{2cm}}$

(e)

$38 - 9 = \underline{\hspace{2cm}}$

(f)

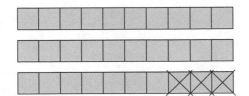

$30 - 3 = \underline{\hspace{2cm}}$

Singapore Math Level 1A & 1B

45. Solve the subtraction problems below by grouping tens and ones.

    (a)   26 – 2 = _____ tens _____ ones – _____ ones

                   = _____ tens _____ ones

                   = _____

    (b)   37 – 3 = _____ tens _____ ones – _____ ones

                   = _____ tens _____ ones

                   = _____

    (c)   16 – 1 = _____ ten _____ ones – _____ one

                   = _____ ten _____ ones

                   = _____

    (d)   24 – 4 = _____ tens _____ ones – _____ ones

                   = _____ tens _____ ones

                   = _____

    (e)   33 – 4 = _____ tens _____ ones – _____ ones

                   = _____ tens _____ ones – _____ ones

                   = _____ tens _____ ones

                   = _____

46. Solve each subtraction problem below.

    (a)   28
          –   7

    (c)   19
          –   6

    (e)   37
          – 13

    (b)   35
          – 12

    (d)   25
          – 11

47. Subtract by regrouping tens and ones.

(a)   3 2
      – 1 8
      ‾‾‾‾‾‾

(c)   2 6
      – 1 7
      ‾‾‾‾‾‾

(e)   3 0
      –   9
      ‾‾‾‾‾‾

(b)   4 0
      – 1 5
      ‾‾‾‾‾‾

(d)   2 3
      – 1 4
      ‾‾‾‾‾‾

48. Match each child to the correct house.

 22    27    32    10    18

36 – 4   28 – 6   17 – 7   34 – 7   22 – 4

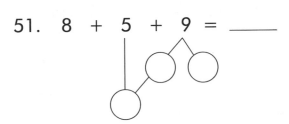

A   B   C   D   E

Fill in each blank with the correct answer.

49. 3 + 5 + 7 = _____

51. 8 + 5 + 9 = _____

50. 4 + 9 + 6 = _____

52. 7 + 6 + 7 = _____

Singapore Math Level 1A & 1B

Add the three numbers in each problem. Write the correct answer on the line.

53. 8 + 6 + 3 = _____

55. 8 + 7 + 6 = _____

54. 9 + 4 + 5 = _____

56. 9 + 6 + 8 = _____

57. Solve the problems listed below. Write your answers in words in the crossword puzzle.

Across

1. 13 – 5

3. 8 – 3

4. 6 + 6

5. 12 – 9

6. 10 + 5

7. 18 – 9

Down

1. 7 + 4

2. 20 – 3

3. 17 – 13

5. 11 + 9

Solve the story problems below. Show your work in the space.

58. Tomás has 21 bookmarks. His mother gives him another 9 bookmarks. How many bookmarks does he have now?

    He has _____ bookmarks now.

59. Charlotte has 35 stickers. She gives 19 stickers to her sister. How many stickers does she have left in the end?

    She has _____ stickers left in the end.

60. Uncle Donald has 26 eggs on his farm. Uncle Jack has 8 fewer eggs than Uncle Donald. How many eggs does Uncle Jack have?

    Uncle Jack has _____ eggs.

61. Zoe has 16 pencils. Parker has 14 pencils more than Zoe. How many pencils does Parker have?

    Parker has _____ pencils.

Unit 13: MENTAL CALCULATIONS

Examples:

1. Add 13 and 5 mentally.

$$3 + 5 = 8$$
$$10 + 8 = 18$$
$$13 + 5 = \underline{18}$$

2. Subtract 9 from 29 mentally.

$$9 - 9 = 0$$
$$20 + 0 = 20$$
$$29 - 9 = \underline{20}$$

Add mentally.

1. $3 + 12 =$ _____

2. $2 + 17 =$ _____

3. $11 + 5 =$ _____

4. $25 + 4 =$ _____

5. $17 + 10 =$ _____

6. $22 + 7 =$ _____

7. $32 + 6 =$ _____

8. $29 + 10 =$ _____

9. $8 + 30 =$ _____

10. $14 + 3 =$ _____

11. $6 + 20 =$ _____

12. $15 + 3 =$ _____

13. $21 + 6 =$ _____

14. $33 + 4 =$ _____

Singapore Math Level 1A & 1B

15. $10 + 9 = $ _____

16. $27 + 2 = $ _____

17. $16 + 10 = $ _____

18. $7 + 11 = $ _____

19. $13 + 6 = $ _____

20. $20 + 2 = $ _____

Subtract mentally.

21. $18 - 3 = $ _____

22. $28 - 6 = $ _____

23. $15 - 5 = $ _____

24. $36 - 4 = $ _____

25. $14 - 10 = $ _____

26. $33 - 2 = $ _____

27. $16 - 3 = $ _____

28. $19 - 5 = $ _____

29. $24 - 4 = $ _____

30. $33 - 30 = $ _____

31. $39 - 20 = $ _____

32. $29 - 4 = $ _____

33. $17 - 2 = $ _____

34. $39 - 3 = $ _____

35. $23 - 2 = $ _____

36. $14 - 3 = $ _____

37. $28 - 10 = $ _____

38. $35 - 4 = $ _____

39. $37 - 10 = $ _____

40. $25 - 3 = $ _____

Unit 14: MULTIPLYING

Example:

Aunt Jess has 6 bags of cherries. There are 2 cherries in each bag. How many cherries does she have altogether?

She has 6 bags of cherries.

Each bag has 2 cherries.

$6 \times 2 = 12$

She has **12** cherries altogether.

Study the pictures below. Fill in each blank with the correct answer.

1.

___ + ___ + ___ = _____

____ fives = _____

2.

___ + ___ + ___ + ___ = _____

____ threes = _____

3.

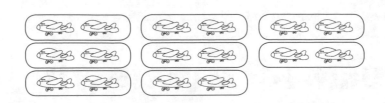

____ + ____ + ____ + ____ + ____ + ____ + ____ + ____ = _____

____ twos = _____

4.

____ + ____ + ____ + ____ + ____ = _____

____ fives = _____

5.

3 _____ = _____

_____ groups of 6 = _____

6.

2 _____ = _____

_____ groups of 10 = _____

7.

7 _____ = _____

_____ groups of 4 = _____

Singapore Math Level 1A & 1B

8.

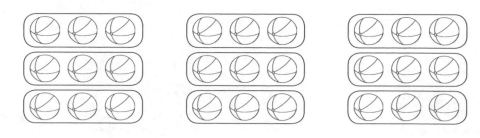

9 _____ = _____

_____ groups of 3 = _____

9.

4 _____ = _____

_____ groups of 9 = _____

10.

10 _____ = _____

_____ groups of 2 = _____

Fill in each blank with the correct answer.

11.

(a)   There are _____ groups of sunflowers.

(b)   There are _____ sunflowers in each group.

(c)   There are _____ sunflowers altogether.

Singapore Math Level 1A & 1B

12.

- (a) There are _____ groups of monkeys.

- (b) There are _____ monkeys in each group.

- (c) There are _____ monkeys altogether.

13.

- (a) There are _____ groups of bread.

- (b) There are _____ pieces of bread in each group.

- (c) There are _____ pieces of bread altogether.

14.

- (a) There are _____ groups of cups.

- (b) There are _____ cups in each group.

- (c) There are _____ cups altogether.

Singapore Math Level 1A & 1B

15.

(a) There are _____ groups of girls.

(b) There are _____ girls in each group.

(c) There are _____ girls altogether.

Study the pictures. Fill in each blank with the correct answer.

16.

_____ groups of _____ socks

_____ × _____ = _____

17.

_____ groups of _____ kiwis

_____ × _____ = _____

18.

_____ groups of _____ children

_____ × _____ = _____

Singapore Math Level 1A & 1B

19.

_____ groups of _____ watches

_____ × _____ = _____

20.

_____ groups of _____ houses

_____ × _____ = _____

Solve the following story problems.

21.

There are 4 vases. There are 5 flowers in each vase. How many flowers are there altogether?

_____ × _____ = _____

There are _____ flowers altogether.

22.

There are 8 baskets. There are 3 pieces of fruit in each basket. How many pieces of fruit are there altogether?

_____ × _____ = _____

There are _____ pieces of fruit altogether.

Singapore Math Level 1A & 1B

23.

There are 3 fish tanks in a shop. There are 6 fish in each tank. How many fish are there altogether?

_____ × _____ = _____

There are _____ fish altogether.

24.

There are 8 horses on a farm. Each horse has 4 legs. How many legs does the group of horses have altogether?

_____ × _____ = _____

The group of horses has _____ legs altogether.

25.

Kimiko has 5 flags. There are 3 stars on each flag. How many stars are there altogether?

_____ × _____ = _____

There are _____ stars altogether.

26.

There are 4 plates on the table. There are 5 pieces of cake on each plate. How many pieces of cake are there altogether?

_____ × _____ = _____

There are _____ pieces of cake altogether.

27.

Jamila has 9 pairs of earrings. Each pair has 2 earrings. How many earrings does Jamila have altogether?

_____ × _____ = _____

Jamila has _____ earrings altogether.

28.

There are 4 trees in a garden. Liam sees 7 birds on each tree. How many birds does Liam see altogether?

_____ × _____ = _____

Liam sees _____ birds altogether.

29.

There are 3 groups of boys on a field. There are 4 boys in each group. How many boys are there altogether?

_____ × _____ = _____

There are _____ boys altogether.

30.

Beatriz has 2 bags of lollipops. There are 8 lollipops in each bag. How many lollipops does Beatriz have altogether?

_____ × _____ = _____

Beatriz has _____ lollipops altogether.

Singapore Math Level 1A & 1B

REVIEW 6

1. Write the numbers on the lines.

   (a) twelve   _____

   (b) twenty-eight   _____

   (c) thirty-five   _____

   (d) eleven   _____

   (e) sixteen   _____

2. Write the following numbers in words.

   (a) 40 _____

   (b) 29 _____

   (c) 13 _____

   (d) 38 _____

   (e) 15 _____

Fill in each blank with the correct answer.

3. 5 less than 20 is _____.   6. 4 more than 15 is _____.

4. 1 more than 39 is _____.   7. 2 less than 17 is _____.

5. 3 less than 27 is _____.

Study the pictures. Fill in each blank with the correct answer.

8.

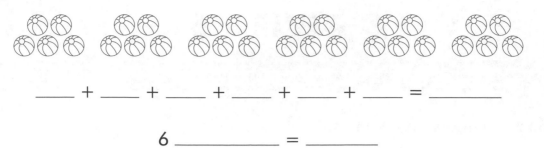

___ + ___ + ___ + ___ + ___ + ___ = _____

6 _____ = _____

9.

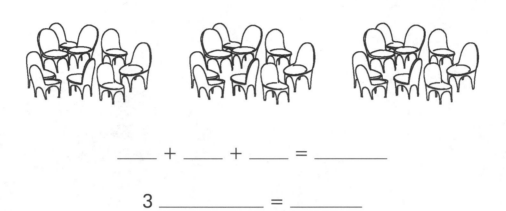

___ + ___ + ___ = _____

3 _____ = _____

10. Fill in each blank with the correct answer.

16	28	19	25	31

(a) The smallest number is _____.

(b) The largest number is _____.

(c) _____ is 3 more than 25.

(d) _____ is 3 less than 22.

(e) _____ is greater than 19 but smaller than 28.

Singapore Math Level 1A & 1B

11. Solve the following problems by grouping tens and ones.

    (a) 36 – 6 = _____ tens _____ ones – _____ ones

                 = _____ tens _____ ones

                 = _____

    (b) 27 – 9 = _____ tens _____ ones – _____ ones

                 = _____ ten _____ ones – _____ ones

                 = _____ ten _____ ones

                 = _____

    (c) 16 – 7 = _____ ten _____ ones – _____ ones

                 = _____ ten _____ ones – _____ ones

                 = _____ tens _____ ones

                 = _____

12. Complete the number patterns.

    (a) _____, 12, 16, 20, _____

    (b) _____, _____, 25, 28, 31

13. Solve each addition problem below.

    (a)   12
       + 24
       ————

    (c)   25
       + 6
       ————

    (b)   15
       + 13
       ————

    (d)   19
       + 17
       ————

14. Solve each subtraction problem below.

(a)
$$\begin{array}{r} 19 \\ -8 \\ \hline \end{array}$$

(c)
$$\begin{array}{r} 40 \\ -\,15 \\ \hline \end{array}$$

(b)
$$\begin{array}{r} 27 \\ -\,14 \\ \hline \end{array}$$

(d)
$$\begin{array}{r} 35 \\ -\,19 \\ \hline \end{array}$$

15. Add 31 and 7 mentally. _____

16. Subtract 10 from 28 mentally. _____

17. 5 + 8 + 4 = _____

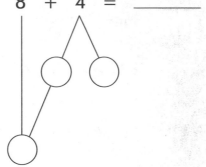

Solve the following story problems. Show your work.

18. George has 24 seashells. He gives 8 shells to his best friend. How many shells does George have left?

□ ○ □ = □

George has _____ seashells left.

Singapore Math Level 1A & 1B

19. Mom bought 3 bags of crackers. There were 7 packages of crackers in each bag. How many packages of crackers were there altogether?

☐ ◯ ☐ = ☐

There were _____ packages of crackers altogether.

20. Madeline buys 8 bunches of bananas in a market. There are 4 bananas in each bunch. How many bananas are there altogether?

☐ ◯ ☐ = ☐

There are _____ bananas altogether.

Singapore Math Level 1A & 1B

Unit 15: DIVIDING

Fill in each blank with the correct answer.

1.

    (a) There are _____ flowers altogether.

    (b) There are _____ vases.

    (c) Place an equal number of flowers in each vase.

    There are _____ flowers in each vase.

2.

(a) There are _____ apples altogether.

(b) There are _____ baskets.

(c) Place an equal number of apples in each basket.

There are _____ apples in each basket.

3. There are 12 socks. Circle 3 equal groups.

There are _____ socks in each group.

4. There are 10 crabs. Circle 2 equal groups.

There are _____ crabs in each group.

5. There are 8 watches. Circle 4 equal groups.

There are _____ watches in each group.

6. There are 18 fish. Place 6 fish into each group.

There are _____ groups of fish.

Singapore Math Level 1A & 1B

7. There are 16 ladybugs. Place 4 ladybugs into each group.

There are _____ groups of ladybugs.

8. There are 20 cakes. Place 2 cakes into each group.

There are _____ groups of cakes.

Solve the following story problems.

9. Mrs. James buys 20 pencils. She gives 4 pencils to each child. How many children are there?

There are _____ children.

10. 3 boys share 12 strawberries equally. How many strawberries does each boy get?

Each boy gets _____ strawberries.

Singapore Math Level 1A & 1B

11. Ms. McKay bakes 18 cupcakes. She gives an equal number of cupcakes to 9 students. How many cupcakes does each student receive?

Each student receives _____ cupcakes.

12. Mr. Ramirez cuts a pizza into 10 slices. The pizza is shared equally among some people. If each person gets 2 slices of pizza, how many people share the pizza?

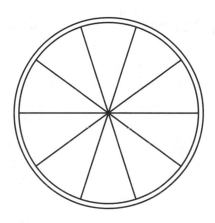

_____ people share the pizza.

Unit 16: TIME

Read the time on each clock. Write the correct time on the lines.

1.

_____

2.

_____

3.

_____

4.

_____

5.

_____

6.

_____

Singapore Math Level 1A & 1B

7.

_____

8.

_____

9.

_____

Match each clock to the correct time.

10.  •

• 5 o'clock, 5:00

11.  •

• 2 o'clock, 2:00

12.  •

• 11 o'clock, 11:00

13.  •

• 4:30

14.  •

• 8:30

15.  •

• 10:30

Singapore Math Level 1A & 1B

Look at the clock in each picture. Fill in each blank with the correct answer.

16.

Anna-Maria has her breakfast at

_____ in the morning.

17.

John and his family have their dinner

at _____ in the evening.

18.

Samantha takes her dog for a walk

at _____ in the evening.

Singapore Math Level 1A & 1B

19.

Colton has to feed his fish at

_____ every evening.

20.

Elizabeth goes to bed at

_____ every night.

21.

Brady walks to school at

_____.

REVIEW 7

Write the correct time on the lines below.

1.

   _____

2.

   _____

3.

   _____

4.

   _____

5.

   _____

6.

   _____

Fill in each blank with the correct answer.

7.

Molly has 18 bars of chocolate. She gives equal numbers of chocolate bars to her

6 friends. Each friend receives _____ bars of chocolate.

Singapore Math Level 1A & 1B

8. There are 20 apples.
   Place 4 apples on each plate.

There are _____ plates of apples.

9. There are 18 bows. Each girl has 3 bows.

There are _____ girls.

10. There are 16 balloons. Each child has 4 balloons.

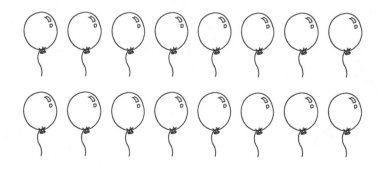

There are _____ children.

Singapore Math Level 1A & 1B

Fill in the correct time on the lines below.

11.

Yoko goes to the library

at _____.

12.

Chris goes to school

at _____.

13.

Mom wakes up

at _____.

14.

Eli eats his lunch

at _____.

15.

Kaitlyn sleeps at _____.

16.

Anthony goes to the park

at _____.

Singapore Math Level 1A & 1B

Solve the following story problems.

17. Winnie has 20 stickers. She gives an equal number of stickers to 5 of her friends. How many stickers does each friend receive?

Each friend receives _____ stickers.

18. Raj and his 2 friends caught 18 fish. They shared the fish equally. How many fish did each boy get?

Each boy got _____ fish.

Singapore Math Level 1A & 1B

19. Billy has 16 toy soldiers. He wants to put an equal number of toy soldiers into 2 boxes. How many toy soldiers are there in each box?

There are _____ toy soldiers in each box.

20. Alexandra buys 20 flowers. She places 4 flowers into each vase. How many vases does she need?

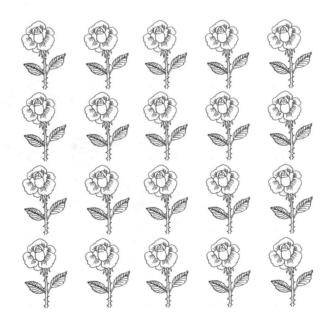

She needs _____ vases.

Singapore Math Level 1A & 1B

Unit 17: NUMBERS 1–100

Examples:

1.

| 92 | 78 | 60 | 43 |

   (a) The largest number is **92**.

   (b) The smallest number is **43**.

   (c) **60** is greater than 43 but smaller than 78.

   (d) **78** is smaller than 92 but greater than 60.

2. Add 81 and 15.

$$81 + 15 = \underline{96}$$

Tens	Ones
8	1
+ 1	5
9	6

3. What is 79 − 34?

$$79 - 34 = \underline{45}$$

Tens	Ones
7	9
− 3	4
4	5

4. What is 81 − 49?

$$81 - 49 = \underline{32}$$

Tens	Ones
⁷8	¹¹1
− 4	9
3	2

Fill in each blank with the correct answer.

1. Write the following numbers in words.

    (a) 75 _____

    (b) 96 _____

    (c) 63 _____

    (d) 55 _____

    (e) 81 _____

    (f) 100 _____

2. Write the numbers on the lines below.

    (a) fifty   _____   (d) eighty-five _____

    (b) ninety-two _____   (e) seventy-six _____

    (c) sixty-four _____   (f) ninety-nine _____

Count the items. Write the correct answer in each blank.

3.

_____ tens _____ ones = _____

_____ + _____ = _____

4.

_____ tens _____ ones = _____

_____ + _____ = _____

5.

_____ tens _____ ones = _____

_____ + _____ = _____

6.

_____ tens _____ ones = _____

_____ + _____ = _____

Singapore Math Level 1A & 1B

7.

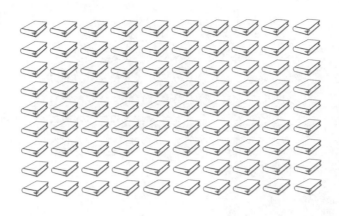

_____ tens _____ ones = _____

_____ + _____ = _____

Fill in each blank with the correct answer.

8. (a)   5 more than 68 is _____.

    (b)   3 less than 75 is _____.

    (c)   4 less than 98 is _____.

    (d)   8 more than 53 is _____.

    (e)   6 more than 82 is _____.

    (f)   7 less than 59 is _____.

    (g)   6 less than 56 is _____.

9.
49	63	57	74	88

(a)   The smallest number is _____.

(b)   The largest number is _____.

(c)   _____ is greater than 63 but smaller than _____.

(d)   _____ is greater than 74.

(e)   _____ is smaller than 57.

Singapore Math Level 1A & 1B

10.

| 96 | 76 | 82 | 64 | 79 |

(a)   The largest number is _____.

(b)   The smallest number is _____.

(c)   3 more than 79 is _____.

(d)   _____ is greater than 76 but smaller than 82.

(e)   _____ is greater than 82.

11.   Complete the number patterns.

(a)   80, 84, _____, _____, 96, _____

(b)   66, _____, 72, 75, _____, _____

(c)   _____, _____, 84, 89, 94

Solve the addition problems below by making tens.

12.   (a)

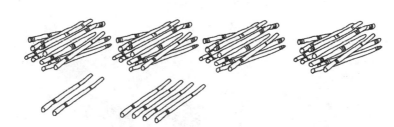

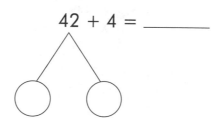

42 + 4 = _____

(b)

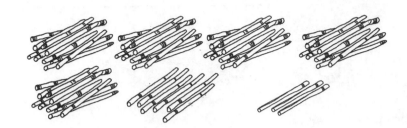

$$56 + 3 = \underline{\hspace{1.5cm}}$$

(c)

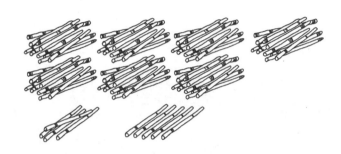

$$74 + 5 = \underline{\hspace{1.5cm}}$$

(d)

$$35 + 30 = \underline{\hspace{1.5cm}}$$

Singapore Math Level 1A & 1B

(e)

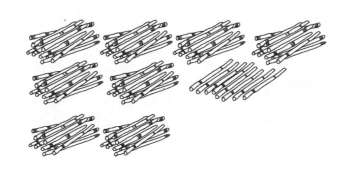

$$68 + 20 = \underline{}$$

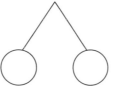

(f)

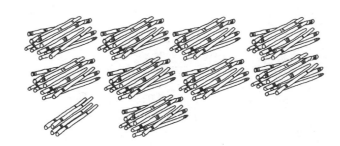

$$84 + 10 = \underline{}$$

Solve these addition problems by first grouping tens and ones.

13. (a) $37 + 8 = \underline{}$ tens $\underline{}$ ones $+ \underline{}$ ones

   $= \underline{}$ tens $\underline{}$ ones

   Regroup the ones.

   $= \underline{}$ tens $\underline{}$ ones

   $= \underline{}$

Singapore Math Level 1A & 1B

(b) $45 + 5$ = _____ tens _____ ones + _____ ones

            = _____ tens _____ ones

            Regroup the ones.

            = _____ tens _____ ones

            = _____

(c) $63 + 9$ = _____ tens _____ ones + _____ ones

            = _____ tens _____ ones

            Regroup the ones.

            = _____ tens _____ ones

            = _____

(d) $74 + 13$ = _____ tens _____ ones + _____ ones

            = _____ tens _____ ones

            Regroup the ones.

            = _____ tens _____ ones

            = _____

(e) $86 + 14$ = _____ tens _____ ones + _____ ones

            = _____ tens _____ ones

            Regroup the ones.

            = _____ tens _____ ones

            = _____

(f) $58 + 22$ = _____ tens _____ ones + _____ ones

            = _____ tens _____ ones

            Regroup the ones.

            = _____ tens _____ ones

            = _____

Singapore Math Level 1A & 1B

14. (a)
```
    53
+   14
_____
```

(e)
```
    28
+   64
_____
```

(b)
```
    70
+   28
_____
```

(f)
```
    35
+   47
_____
```

(c)
```
    91
+    6
_____
```

(g)
```
    68
+   18
_____
```

(d)
```
    44
+   34
_____
```

(h)
```
    86
+    9
_____
```

15. Match each cyclist to the correct bicycle.

A

67 + 20

•

B

62 + 14

•

C

46 + 3

•

D

53 + 18

•

•

49

•

71

•

87

•

76

Solve these subtraction problems by first grouping tens and ones.

16. (a)   64 – 3 = _____

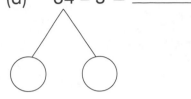

(d)   77 – 5 = _____

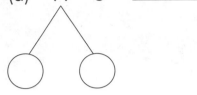

(b)   89 – 6 = _____

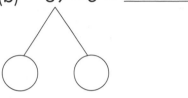

(e)   54 – 6 = _____

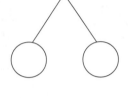

(c)   93 – 4 = _____

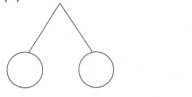

17. (a)   45 – 3 = _____ tens _____ ones – _____ ones

= _____ tens _____ ones

= _____

(b)   68 – 7 = _____ tens _____ ones – _____ ones

= _____ tens _____ one

= _____

(c)   76 – 6 = _____ tens _____ ones – _____ ones

= _____ tens _____ ones

= _____

(d)   95 – 20 = _____ tens _____ ones – _____ tens

= _____ tens _____ ones

= _____

Singapore Math Level 1A & 1B

(e) 84 – 30 = _____ tens _____ ones – _____ tens

          = _____ tens _____ ones

          = _____

(f) 93 – 12 = _____ tens _____ ones – _____ ten _____ ones

          = _____ tens _____ one

          = _____

(g) 56 – 17 = _____ tens _____ ones – _____ ten _____ ones

          = _____ tens _____ ones – _____ ten _____ ones

          = _____ tens _____ ones

          = _____

18. (a)
$$\begin{array}{r} 97 \\ -\ 36 \\ \hline \end{array}$$

(b)
$$\begin{array}{r} 78 \\ -\ 12 \\ \hline \end{array}$$

(c)
$$\begin{array}{r} 46 \\ -\ 25 \\ \hline \end{array}$$

(d)
$$\begin{array}{r} 89 \\ -\ 54 \\ \hline \end{array}$$

(e)
$$\begin{array}{r} 60 \\ -\ 37 \\ \hline \end{array}$$

(f)
$$\begin{array}{r} 55 \\ -\ 28 \\ \hline \end{array}$$

(g)
$$\begin{array}{r} 92 \\ -\ 46 \\ \hline \end{array}$$

(h)
$$\begin{array}{r} 71 \\ -\ 17 \\ \hline \end{array}$$

19. Match each helmet to the correct child.

·   ·   ·   ·

·   ·   ·   ·

Solve the story problems below.

20. Jake has 80 toy soldiers. Demetrius has 10 fewer toy soldiers. How many toy soldiers does Demetrius have?

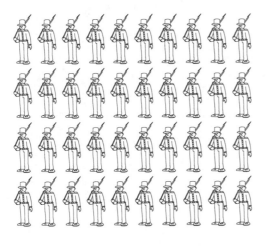 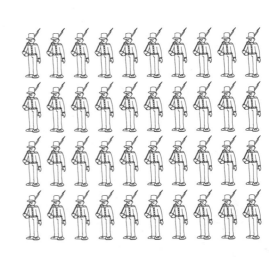

Demetrius has _____ toy soldiers.

21. Chloe collects 65 stamps. Rachel collects 8 fewer stamps. How many stamps does Rachel collect?

Rachel collects _____ stamps.

22. Logan has 72 bottle caps. He has 18 fewer bottle caps than Justin. How many bottle caps does Justin have?

Justin has _____ bottle caps.

23. Sasha has 18 stickers. Akira has 10 fewer stickers than Sasha. Julia has 3 stickers more than Akira.

(a) How many stickers does Akira have?

$$\boxed{} \bigcirc \boxed{} = \boxed{}$$

Akira has _____ stickers.

(b) How many stickers does Julia have?

$$\boxed{} \bigcirc \boxed{} = \boxed{}$$

Julia has _____ stickers.

(c) Who has the fewest stickers?

_____ has the fewest stickers.

Unit 18: MONEY (PART 1)

Examples:

1. Erika wants to exchange $2.00 for some fifty-cent coins. How many fifty-cent coins will she receive?

    | $1 | $1 | = 50¢ 50¢ 50¢ 50¢

    She will receive **4** fifty-cent coins.

2. Vincent uses the money shown below to buy a burger. How much does the burger cost?

    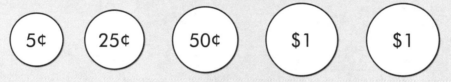

    The burger costs **$2.80**.

Fill in each blank with the correct answer.

1. 50¢ = _____ ten-cent coins

2. $1 = _____ fifty-cent coins

3. $5 = _____ one-dollar coins

4. $10 = _____ five-dollar bills

5. 10¢ = _____ five-cent coins

6. $50 = _____ ten-dollar bills

Singapore Math Level 1A & 1B

7. $2 = _____ fifty-cent coins

8. $1 = _____ twenty-five-cent coins

9. $50 = _____ five-dollar bills

10. $1 = _____ five-cent coins

Study the pictures carefully. Write the correct amount of money in the boxes.

11. $10 $5 $1	
12. $10 $10 $5 $5	
13. $50 $10 $1 $5 $1	
14. $50 $5 $1 $1 $1	

Singapore Math Level 1A & 1B

15.

| $10 | $5 | $1 | $1 |
| $5 | $5 | $1 | $1 |

16.

50¢ 25¢ 10¢ 5¢

17.

50¢ 25¢ 10¢ 10¢

18.

25¢ 25¢ 10¢ 5¢

19.

50¢ 25¢ 10¢ 5¢ 5¢ 5¢

20.

25¢ 10¢ 10¢

Look at each picture, and color the amount of money you would need to purchase the item shown.

21. $6	$10 $10 $5 $5 $1 $1	
22. $19	$10 $10 $1 $5 $5 $1 $1 $1	
23. $25	$10 $10 $5 $1 $1 $1 $1	
24. $4	$5 $5 $1 $1 $1 $1 $1	
25. $36	$10 $10 $1 $10 $5 $5	

Singapore Math Level 1A & 1B

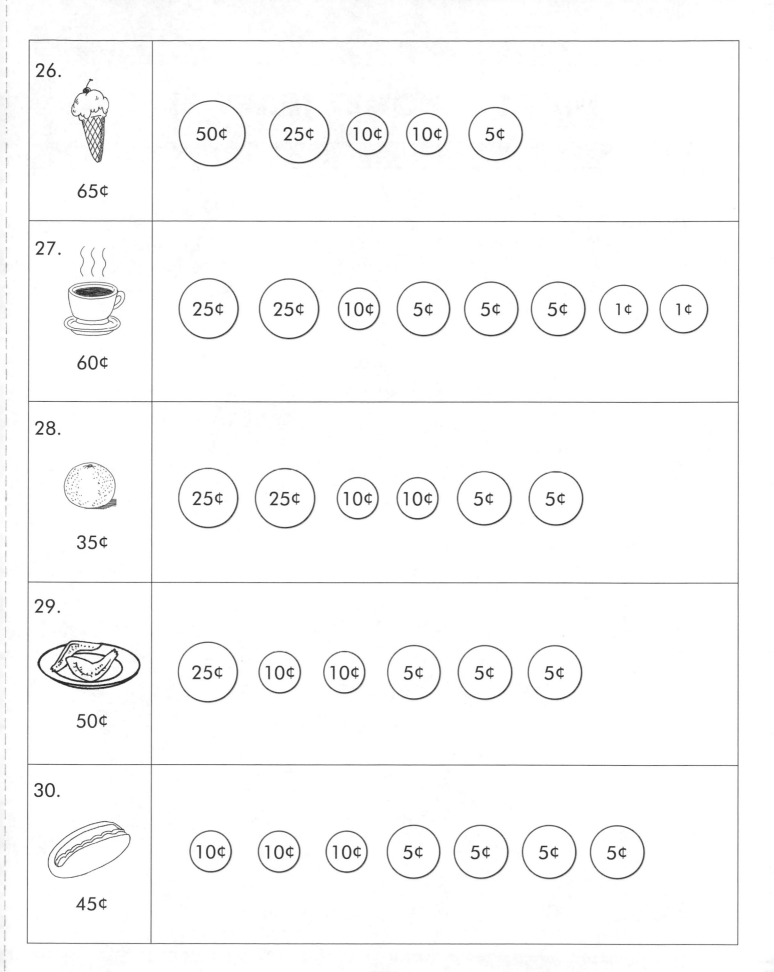

26.

65¢

50¢   25¢   10¢   10¢   5¢

27.

60¢

25¢   25¢   10¢   5¢   5¢   5¢   1¢   1¢

28.

35¢

25¢   25¢   10¢   10¢   5¢   5¢

29.

50¢

25¢   10¢   10¢   5¢   5¢   5¢

30.

45¢

10¢   10¢   10¢   5¢   5¢   5¢   5¢

Singapore Math Level 1A & 1B

Unit 19: MONEY (PART 2)

Examples:

1. Angelo buys 2 pieces of fruit in the school cafeteria.
    A piece of watermelon costs 50¢.
    An orange costs 30¢ more than the watermelon.
    How much is the orange?

    $$50¢ + 30¢ = 80¢$$

    The orange is **80¢**.

2. Noelle buys a skirt that costs $38.
    She gives the cashier $50.
    How much change will she receive?

    $$\$50 - \$38 = \$12$$

    She will receive **$12**.

Study the pictures below. Fill in each blank with the correct answer.

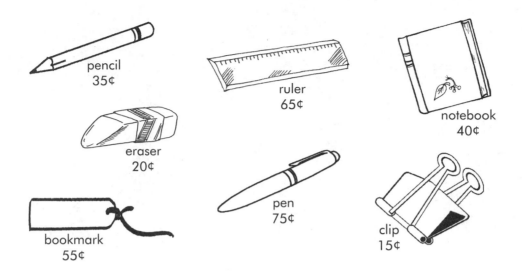

pencil
35¢

ruler
65¢

notebook
40¢

eraser
20¢

pen
75¢

bookmark
55¢

clip
15¢

1. Mariah buys the eraser and the notebook.

    How much does she spend altogether? _____

2. Ryan buys the bookmark and the notebook.

    How much does he pay for both items? _____

3. Stella buys the clip. She gives the cashier 50¢.

    How much change will she get? _____

4. Layla wants to buy the pen and the pencil.

    How much will she pay for the 2 items? _____

5. Mateo has 80¢. He wants to buy 2 items. Which 2 items can he buy that total exactly 80¢?

    _____ and _____

Look at the items sold at a toy store. Study the pictures below, and fill in each blank with the correct answer.

6. Sean wants to buy the toy monkey and the pack of playing cards.

   How much must he pay altogether?   _____

7. How much more does the toy car cost than the doll?   _____

8. Xavier wants the toy plane and the toy helicopter for his birthday.

   How much do the 2 toys cost altogether?   _____

9. Katherine has $50. She wants to buy the toy monkey.

   How much change will she receive?   _____

10. Ada buys 2 items for $25. What are the 2 items?

                              _____ and _____

Singapore Math Level 1A & 1B

Below are some items sold in a department store. Study the pictures, and fill in each blank with the correct answer.

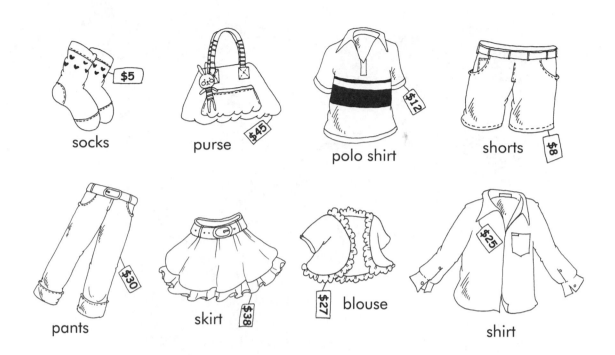

socks — $5
purse — $45
polo shirt — $12
shorts — $8
pants — $30
skirt — $38
blouse — $27
shirt — $25

11. Luis bought the pair of socks and the shirt.
     How much did he pay?   _____

12. How much more does the skirt cost than the pair of pants?   _____

13. Andrea bought the polo shirt and the pair of shorts.
     How much did she pay altogether?   _____

14. Fatima had $20. She wanted to buy the purse.
     How much more money did she need?   _____

15. Emma wanted to buy 2 items. She had $65.
     What could she buy that would total exactly $65?

                                    _____ and _____

Below are the items sold in Mr. Angley's store. Study the pictures, and fill in each blank with the correct answer.

beach ball $8
bag $20
beach umbrella $33
bathing suit $25
mat $13
sandals $5
swimming trunks $12
float $16

16. June buys the bathing suit and the pair of sandals.

    How much does she pay altogether? _____

17. Bryan buys 2 items and pays $29 for them.

    What are the 2 items? _____ and _____

18. Christine buys the bag and the swimming trunks for her brother.

    How much does she pay in all? _____

19. Khalid wants to buy the mat. He has only $10.

    How much more money does he need? _____

20. How much less do the swimming trunks cost than the bathing suit?

    _____

Singapore Math Level 1A & 1B

Solve the following story problems. Show your work in the space below.

21. Mala has $28. Her father gives her another $15. How much money does she have now?

22. Grace has $90. She lends $32 to her classmate. How much money does she have left?

23. Frankie buys an eraser for 60¢ and a ruler for 25¢. How much does he spend in all?

24. Nelson has a daily allowance of 90¢. He spends 55¢ and saves the rest of his money. How much does he save every day?

25. Grandmother spends $34 on gas every week. She also spends $55 on food. How much does she spend altogether in a week?

Singapore Math Level 1A & 1B

REVIEW 8

1. Fill in each blank with the correct answer.

36	79	56	64	59

(a) The smallest number is _____.

(b) The largest number is _____.

(c) _____ is 3 more than 56.

(d) _____ is 3 less than 59.

(e) _____ is greater than 59 but smaller than 79.

Match the following amounts on the left to the correct totals on the right.

2. 4 twenty-five-cent coins •   • $25

3. 3 ten-cent coins •   • $1

4. 2 ten-dollar bills •   • 30¢

5. 5 five-dollar bills •   • $20

6. 6 ten-dollar bills •   • $60

Singapore Math Level 1A & 1B

Solve the addition and subtraction problems below.

7. (a)   8 3
        + 1 5
        ——————

    (b)   4 6
        + 1 2
        ——————

    (c)   3 8
        + 3 6
        ——————

    (d)   7 7
        + 2 3
        ——————

8. (a)   9 5
        − 4 3
        ——————

    (b)   6 8
        − 2 6
        ——————

    (c)   5 0
        − 2 8
        ——————

    (d)   8 3
        − 4 7
        ——————

Color the amount of money you would need to buy each item shown.

9.

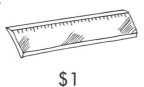

$3

$1 $1

50¢   25¢   25¢   10¢   10¢

10.

$1

50¢   50¢   25¢   10¢   10¢

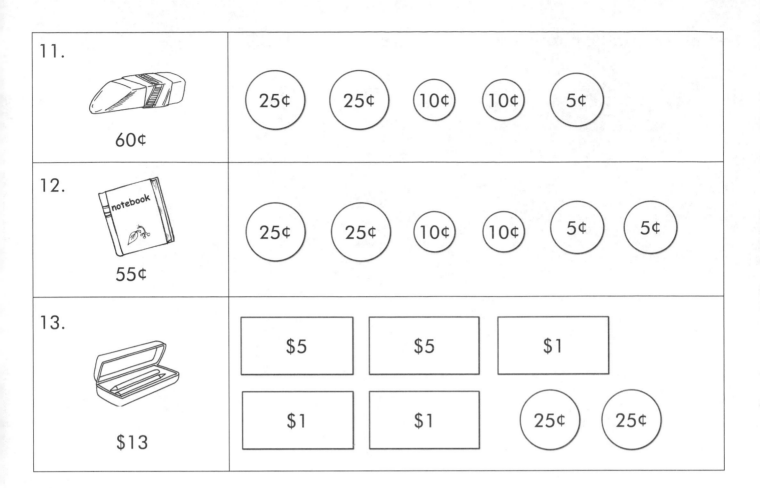

11. 60¢	25¢ 25¢ 10¢ 10¢ 5¢
12. notebook 55¢	25¢ 25¢ 10¢ 10¢ 5¢ 5¢
13. $13	$5 $5 $1 $1 $1 25¢ 25¢

14. Complete the number pattern.

61, _____, _____, 82, 89

Solve the story problems below. Show your work in the space.

15. Nadya has 15 hair clips. Ali has 30 hair clips. How many hair clips do they have altogether?

[ ] ◯ [ ] = [ ]

They have _____ hair clips altogether.

Singapore Math Level 1A & 1B

16. Alex saves $25. Jorge saves $15 more than Alex. P.J. saves $9 less than Jorge.

 (a) How much does Jorge save?

$$\boxed{} \bigcirc \boxed{} = \boxed{}$$

 Jorge saves $_____.

 (b) How much does P.J. save?

$$\boxed{} \bigcirc \boxed{} = \boxed{}$$

 P.J. saves $_____.

17. Peyton buys 30 baseball cards. Tom buys 10 fewer cards than Peyton. How many baseball cards does Tom buy?

$$\boxed{} \bigcirc \boxed{} = \boxed{}$$

 Tom buys _____ baseball cards.

18. There are 6 students in Group A, 5 students in Group B, and 9 students in Group C. How many students are there altogether?

$$\boxed{} \bigcirc \boxed{} \bigcirc \boxed{} = \boxed{}$$

 There are _____ students altogether.

Singapore Math Level 1A & 1B

19. Dominique wants to buy 2 toys at the store. She has $50.

(a) How much do the toys cost?

 $\bigcirc$ $=$

The toys cost $_____.

(b) How much change will Dominique receive?

 $\bigcirc$  $=$

She will receive $_____ in change.

20. Caleb has 1 ten-dollar bill. He wants to exchange it for some five-dollar bills. How many five-dollar bills will Caleb receive?

Caleb will receive _____ five-dollar bills.

Singapore Math Level 1A & 1B

FINAL REVIEW

Fill in each blank with the correct answer.

1.

There are _____ fewer butterflies than flowers.

2.   A fifty-cent coin can be exchanged for _____ ten-cent coins.

3. $3 + 3 + 3 + 3 + 3$ is the same as _____ threes.

Fill in the blanks with lighter than, heavier than, **or** as heavy as.

4.

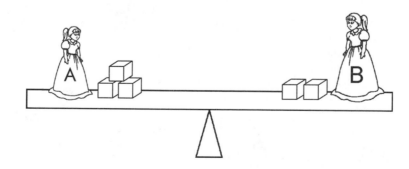

Doll A is _____ Doll B.

5.

Dad goes to work at _____
every morning.

6. Use 3 numbers to complete the number sentence below. Use numbers from the box only ONCE.

2	3	4	6	9

_____ × _____ = _____

Study the pictures below. Write the correct number sentences.

7. (a)

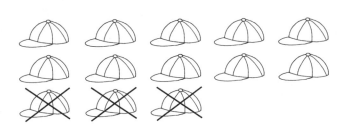

_____ – _____ = _____

(b)

_____ + _____ = _____

Singapore Math Level 1A & 1B

The picture graph below shows the number of books Sadie read in 4 months. Study the picture graph. Answer the questions.

8.

January	📖 📖 📖 📖
February	📖 📖 📖 📖 📖 📖 📖 📖 📖
March	📖 📖 📖 📖 📖 📖 📖 📖
April	📖 📖 📖 📖 📖 📖

Each 📖 stands for 1 book.

(a) Sadie read the most books in _____.

(b) Sadie read the fewest books in _____.

(c) Sadie read _____ more book(s) in February than in March.

(d) Sadie read _____ fewer books in January than in April.

(e) Sadie read _____ books altogether in 4 months.

Fill in each blank with the correct answer.

9. 10 less than 88 is _____.

10. Subtract 34 from 74 mentally. _____

11.

Joey has $_____.

12. Amanda had 90¢. She bought a pair of scissors for 60¢.

    She had _____¢ left.

13. There are 15 beetles. Circle the beetles in groups of 3.

    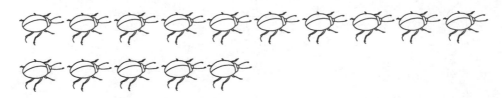

    There are _____ groups of beetles.

14.

    School ends at _____ today.

15. Arrange the numbers in order. Begin with the smallest.

    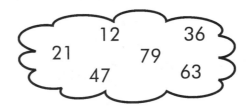

    _____, _____, _____, _____, _____, _____

16.

49	36	73	68

    (a) The smallest number is _____.

    (b) The largest number is _____.

Singapore Math Level 1A & 1B

17.

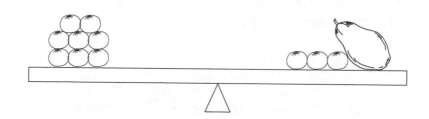

The squash has the same mass as _____ oranges.

18.

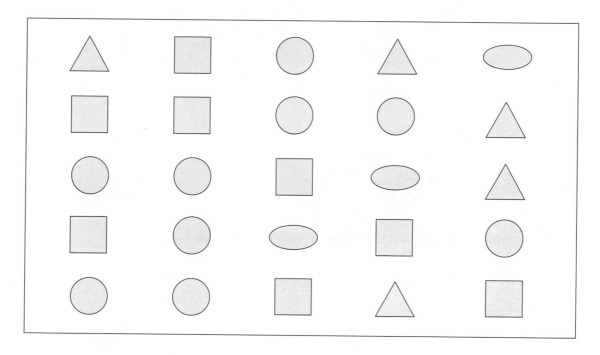

Study the shapes above, and complete the picture graph below.

Triangle	
Square	
Circle	
Oval	
	Each ☆ stands for 1 shape.

Fill in the blanks with the correct answers.

19.

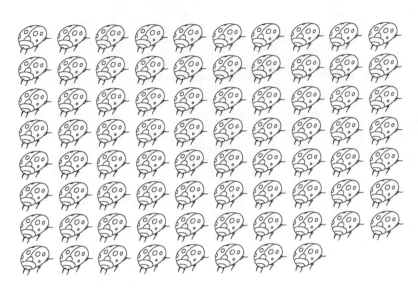

_____ tens _____ ones = _____

Solve the following story problems. Show your work.

20. Colby goes to the store with 45¢. A notebook costs 75¢. How much more money does he need?

☐ ◯ ☐ = ☐

He needs _____¢ more.

21. Mom puts 2 sandwiches in each box. How many sandwiches are there in 5 boxes?

☐ ◯ ☐ = ☐

There are _____ sandwiches in 5 boxes.

Singapore Math Level 1A & 1B

22. Shawn ate 4 crackers. There were still 18 crackers in the package. How many crackers were there in the beginning?

$$\boxed{} \bigcirc \boxed{} = \boxed{}$$

There were _____ crackers in the beginning.

23. Mrs. Terry bakes 20 muffins. If she packs 4 muffins into each box, how many boxes does she need?

She needs _____ boxes.

24. Bianca had 62 stickers. She gave some to her friends and had 22 stickers left. How many stickers did Bianca give to her friends?

$$\boxed{} \bigcirc \boxed{} = \boxed{}$$

She gave _____ stickers to her friends.

25. Eve has $50. She buys a doll for $38. How much change will she receive?

$$\boxed{} \bigcirc \boxed{} = \boxed{}$$

She will receive $_____ in change.

Singapore Math Level 1A & 1B

CHALLENGE QUESTIONS

Solve the following problems on another sheet of paper.

1. Mrs. Patel goes to the supermarket. She wants to buy 10 kg of sugar. However, the sugar is sold in 1-kg, 2-kg, and 5-kg bags. List 5 ways that she can buy 10 kg of sugar.

2. X is a 2-digit number. The sum of all its digits is 9. The first digit is 3 more than the second digit. What is X?

3. Rico keeps some birds and cats as pets. The total number of legs his animals have is 22. The number of cats is 1 more than the number of birds. How many cats and birds does he have?

4. Clock A chimes every 2 minutes. Clock B chimes every 5 minutes. If the 2 clocks are timed together, how many times will they chime in 10 minutes?

5. Jess has 3 bills of different values. The total value of these bills is $35. What bills does she have?

6. Brianna has 2 watches that are not working well. Watch A is 4 hours fast. Watch B is 8 hours slow. What is the actual time in the morning when both watches show 12:00?

Singapore Math Level 1A & 1B

7. $\heartsuit + \heartsuit + \heartsuit + \triangle + \triangle = 16$

     $\triangle + \triangle + \triangle + \triangle = 20$

What is the value of $\heartsuit$?

8. Kenji flipped to a page in his math workbook. The sum of the facing pages was 61. Which 2 pages was Kenji looking at?

9. I am a 2-digit number. When the first digit is subtracted from the second digit, the result is 7. The first digit is an even number, and the second digit is an odd number. What number am I?

10. Nicky watched a cartoon in the afternoon. It lasted an hour. 5 hours after the cartoon, he went to bed at 9 o'clock. What time did the cartoon start?

11. Elian's mother gave him 2 coins. The sum of the coins was less than a dollar. What was the greatest amount of money that Elian could receive from his mother?

Singapore Math Level 1A & 1B

SOLUTIONS
Singapore Math Level 1A

Unit 1: Numbers 1–10

1. **3**
2. **6**
3. **4**
4. **1**
5. **8**
6. **2**
7. **5**
8. **7**
9. **9**
10. **10**

11. (cat image)
12. (vase of flowers image)
13. (plate of oranges image)
14. (bicycle image)
15. (table image)
16. (three)
17. (eight)
18. (five)
19. (seven)
20. (four)

21.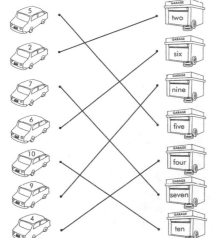

22.	3 apples	(3 apples)
23.	6 balls	(6 balls)
24.	8 fish	(8 fish)
25.	7 stars	(7 stars)
26.	10 pencils	(10 pencils)

27. **more, fewer**
There are 6 boys and 4 bicycles.
28. **flowers, trees**
trees, flowers
There are 3 trees and 6 flowers.

29. **more, fewer**
There are 6 oranges and 4 apples.
30. **fewer, more**
There are 3 shirts and 4 skirts.
31. **boys, girls**
girls, boys
There are 3 girls and 7 boys.
32. (4)
4 is smaller than 6.
33. (8)
8 is smaller than 10.
34. (1)
1 is smaller than 3.
35. (7)
7 is smaller than 9.
36. (2)
2 is smaller than 5.
37. Color **8**
8 is greater than 6.
38. Color **4**
4 is greater than 3.
39. Color **9**
9 is greater than 7.
40. Color **5**
5 is greater than 2.
41. Color **8**
8 is greater than 1.
42. **4, 8**
Count 4, 5, 6, 7, and 8.
43. **3, 4**
Count 2, 3, 4, 5, and 6.
44. **7, 5**
Count 8, 7, 6, 5, and 4.
45. **5, 1**
Count 5, 4, 3, 2, and 1.
46. 2 + 1 = **3**
47. 7 + 1 = **8**
48. 3 + 1 = **4**
49. 1 + 1 = **2**
50. 4 + 1 = **5**
51. 8 + 1 = **9**
52. 5 + 1 = **6**
53. 2 + 1 = **3**
54. 7 − 1 = **6**
55. 4 − 1 = **3**
56. 8 − 1 = **7**
57. 2 − 1 = **1**
58. 3 − 1 = **2**
59. 6 − 1 = **5**
60. 9 − 1 = **8**
61. 5 − 1 = **4**
62. **10, nine, 8, seven, 6, five, 4, three, 2, one, 10**

Singapore Math Level 1A & 1B

1. 4 — 1 / 3

2. 6 — 3 / 3

3. 8 — 3 / 5

4. 5 — 0 / 5

5. 10 — 4 / 6

7. 7 — 5 / 2

8. 10 — 3 / 7

9. 6 — 2 / 4

10. 8 — 0 / 8

11. 9 — 2 / 7

12. 5 — 1 / 4

13. 8 — 2 / 6

14. 10 — 3 / 7

15. 7 — 2 / 5

16.
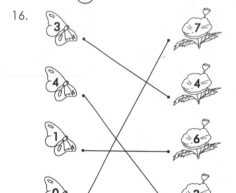

17.
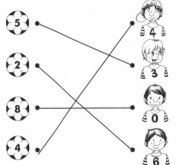

18.
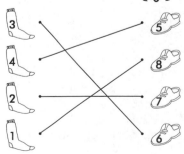

19.
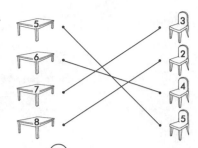

20. 5 — 3 / 2   3 and 2 make 5.

21. 8 — 6 / 2   6 and 2 make 8.

22. 10 — 3 / 7   3 and 7 make 10.

23. 5 — 5 / 0   5 and 0 make 5.

24. 9 — 8 / 1   8 and 1 make 9.

25. 2 — 0 / 2   0 and 2 make 2.

26. 6 — 2 / 4   2 and 4 make 6.

27. 10 — 0 / 10   0 and 10 make 10.

Review 1

1. **8**
2. **2**
3. **9**
4. 9 — 3 / 6

5. 8 — 4 / 4

6.

7.

8.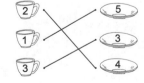

9. (nine)
10. (four)
11. (seven)

12. **more**, **fewer**
There are 8 books and 4 pencils.

13. **ladybugs**, **leaves**
leaves, **ladybugs**
There are 9 ladybugs and 3 leaves.

14. ⑨
9 is greater than 7.

15. ③
3 is smaller than 5.

16. **5, 6**
Count 5, 6, 7, 8, and 9.

17. 1 + 9 = **10**

18. 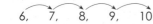   3 and 4 make 7.

19.    1 and 4 make 5.

20. 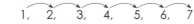   3 and 7 make 10.

Unit 3: Adding Numbers up to 10

1. 4 + **2** = **6**
   4, 5, 6

2. 3 + **5** = **8**
   3, 4, 5, 6, 7, 8

3. 6 + **4** = **10**
   6, 7, 8, 9, 10

4. 2 + **1** = **3**
   2, 3

5. 5 + **4** = **9**
   5, 6, 7, 8, 9

6. **4** + **3** = **7**
   4, 5, 6, 7

7. **3** + **6** = **9**
   3, 4, 5, 6, 7, 8, 9

8. **5** + **5** = **10**
   5, 6, 7, 8, 9, 10

9. **1** + **6** = **7**
   1, 2, 3, 4, 5, 6, 7

10. **4** + **6** = **10**
    4, 5, 6, 7, 8, 9, 10

11. **2** + **5** = **7**
    2, 3, 4, 5, 6, 7

12. **5**
    3, 4, 5

13. **5** + **4** = **9**
    5, 6, 7, 8, 9

14. **6 + 3 = 9**
    6, 7, 8, 9
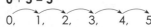

15. **2 + 1 = 3**
    2, 3

16. **0 + 5 = 5**
    0, 1, 2, 3, 4, 5

17. ②─⑤ / ③
5 girls are performing on stage.

18. ④─⑨ / ⑤
There are **9** penguins in all.

19. ②─⑦ / ⑤
There are **7** boys altogether.

20. ④─⑧ / ④
There are **8** flowers altogether.

21. ⑤─⑩ / ⑤
There are **10** rabbits altogether.

22. ⑥ / ② ④
23. ⑦ / ④ ③
24. ⑨ / ④ ⑤
28. ⑧ / ② ⑥
29. ④ / ③ ①

25. ⑦ / ⓪ ⑦
26. ⑥ / ① ⑤
27. ⑩ / ② ⑧
30. ⑦ / ② ⑤
31. ⑨ / ⓪ ⑨

32. [4 + 5]   4 + 5 = 9
33. [7 + 0]   7 + 0 = 7
34. [3 + 2]   3 + 2 = 5
35. [3 + 3]   3 + 3 = 6
36. [0 + 4]   0 + 4 = 4

37. **3** + 6 = 9
3, 4, 5, 6, 7, 8, 9

38. 1 + **7** = 8
1, 2, 3, 4, 5, 6, 7, 8

39. 3 + **2** = 5
3, 4, 5

40. **4** + 4 = 8
4, 5, 6, 7, 8

41. 5 + **1** = 6
5, 6

42. **2** + 7 = 9
2, 3, 4, 5, 6, 7, 8, 9

43. **4** + 6 = 10
4, 5, 6, 7, 8, 9, 10

44. **0** + 3 = 3
0, 1, 2, 3

45. 3 + **4** = 7
3, 4, 5, 6, 7

46. **0** + 2 = 2
0, 1, 2

47. **4 + 2 = 6**
4, 2, 6

48. **5 + 4 = 9**
5, 4, 9

49. **6 + 2 = 8**
6, 2, 8

50. **4 + 5 = 9**, 9
51. **2 + 5 = 7**, 7
52. **3 + 6 = 9**, 9
53. **3, 3, 6, 6**
54. **5 + 2 = 7**, 7
55. **5 + 1 = 6**, 6
56. **4 + 6 = 10, 10**
57. **6 + 1 = 7**, 7

Unit 4: Subtracting Numbers up to 10

1.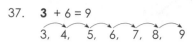
5 – 2 = **3**

2.
10 – 6 = **4**

3.
8 – 3 = **5**

4.
9 – 4 = **5**

5.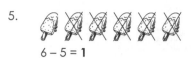
6 – 5 = **1**

6.
7 – 1 = **6**

7.
5 – 0 = **5**

8. ⊗ ⊗ ⊗ ⊗ ⊗ ○ ○ ○
8 – 5 = **3**

9.
7 – 3 = **4**

10.
10 – 7 = **3**

11. **5, 5**
12. **7 – 3 = 4, 4**
13. **10 – 5 = 5, 5**
14. **5 – 0 = 5, 5**
15. **9 – 2 = 7, 7**
16. **6**
3, 4, 5, 6, 7, 8, 9

17. **5**
1, 2, 3, 4, 5, 6

18. **1**
2, 3

19. **2**
6, 7, 8

20. **6**
4, 5, 6, 7, 8, 9, 10

21. **3**
5, 4, 3

22. **5**
10, 9, 8, 7, 6, 5

23. **6**
7, 6

24. **7**
9, 8, 7

25. **1**
4, 3, 2, 1

26. **8** — 2, 6
27. **9** — 3, 6
28. **8** — 4, 4
29. **6** — 2, 4

30.

31.

Diego has **1** toy car left.

32.

Mr. Johnson has **7** telephones left.

33.

2 trains remained at the station.

34.

Ella has **6** starfish left.

35.

There are **2** rocking horses left.

36.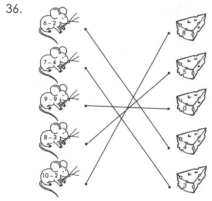

37. **4**
    8, 7, 6, 5, 4

38. **2**

39. **1**
    7, 6, 5, 4, 3, 2, 1

40. **7**
    9, 8, 7

41. **4**
    5, 4

42. **0**
    6, 5, 4, 3, 2, 1, 0

43. **1**
    4, 3, 2, 1

44. **7**
    10, 9, 8, 7

45. **6**
    8, 7, 6

46. **5**
    10, 9, 8, 7, 6, 5

47. **8, 3, 5, 5**
48. **6, 4, 6, 2, 2**
49. **9, 3, 9, 6, 6**
50. **5, 2, 5, 3, 3**
51. **6 − 2 = 4, 4**
52. **10 − 3 = 7, 7**
53. **5 − 3 = 2 , 2**
54. **2 + 6 = 8**
    6 + 2 = 8
    8 − 2 = 6
    8 − 6 = 2

55. **5 + 4 = 9**
    4 + 5 = 9
    9 − 5 = 4
    9 − 4 = 5
56. **3 + 2 = 5**
    2 + 3 = 5
    5 − 3 = 2
    5 − 2 = 3

Review 2

1. **3 + 4 = 7**
   3, 4, 5, 6, 7

2. **2 + 8 = 10**
   2, 3, 4, 5, 6, 7, 8, 9, 10

3.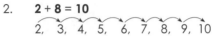
   4 − 4 = **0**

4.
   8 − 6 = **2**

5. **5**

6. **6 − 2 = 4**

7. **9 − 0 = 9**

8. **4 + 5 = 9**

9. **4 + 2 = 6**

10. **7**

11. **0**

12. **7**

231

Singapore Math Level 1A & 1B

13. **9**

14. **6, 3**
    6 + 3 = 9
    9
15. **7, 3**
    7 − 3 = 4
    4
16. **3 + 4 = 7**
    4 + 3 = 7
    7 − 3 = 4
    7 − 4 = 3
17. **7 + 2 = 9, 9**
18. **10 − 5 = 5, $5**
19. **4 + 2 = 6, 6**
20. **8 − 3 = 5, 5**

Unit 5: Shapes and Patterns

1. **circle**
2. **rectangle**
3. **triangle**
4. **square**

5–8.

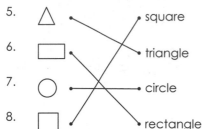

5. △ ⟶ square
6. ▭ ⟶ triangle
7. ○ ⟶ circle
8. □ ⟶ rectangle

9. ◣ ◣ ○ ◿ ▭

10. ⬤ □ ○ ⬤ ▭

11. ▩ ◺ ◻ ○ ▩

12. ▨ ▭ ▨ ○ △

13. [box containing numbered shapes]

14. *Possible answer:*

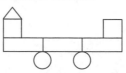

15. Shapes should be colored according to the key.

16. △ □

    A change in shape; △ comes after ○, and □ comes after △ in the pattern.

17. ▭ ▯

    A change in position; ▭ comes after the preceding ▭, and ▯ comes after ▭.

18. ▽ ◣

    A change in types of triangles; ▽ comes after ◢, and ◣ comes after ▽.

19. ▥ ▨

    A change in shapes and sizes; ▥ comes after ☰, and ▨ comes after ▥.

20. ▭ ▯

    A change in position of rectangles and dots; ▭ comes after ▯, and ▯ comes after ▭.

21. ○

    A change in shape; ○ comes after □.

22. ◭

    A change in position of the rectangle in the triangle; ◭ comes after △.

23. ◳

    A change in direction of the shaded box; ⊞ comes after ⊞.

24. ◲

    A change in shape; ◲ comes after ☰.

25. ◁▷

    A change in shape; ◁▷ comes after ⬭.

26. ◻ (the biggest cube)

    A change in size

27. ∇

    A change in direction of the base of the cone; ∇ comes after ◁▷.

28. ▣

    A change in direction of dot on the cube; ▣ comes after ▣.

Singapore Math Level 1A & 1B

Unit 6: Ordinal Numbers

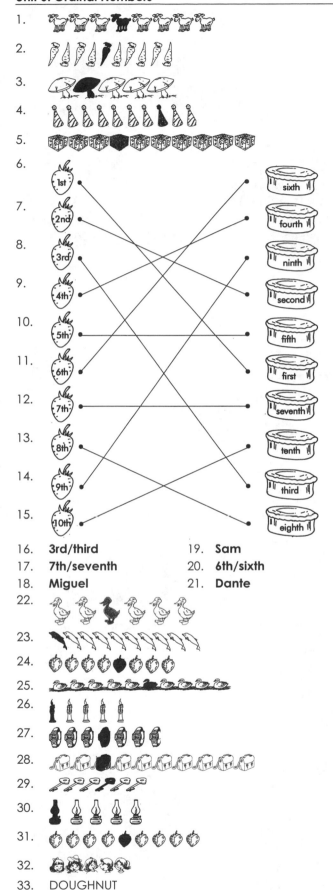

1.
2.
3.
4.
5.
6. 1st — seventh
7. 2nd
8. 3rd
9. 4th
10. 5th
11. 6th
12. 7th
13. 8th
14. 9th
15. 10th

16. **3rd/third**
17. **7th/seventh**
18. **Miguel**
19. **Sam**
20. **6th/sixth**
21. **Dante**

22.
23.
24.
25.
26.
27.
28.
29.
30.
31.
32.
33. DOUGHNUT

Review 3

1.
2. tr**ian**gle
3. re**cta**ngle
4. **sixth**
5. **1st**
6. **3rd**
7. **eighth**

8. ☐○△
A change in shape; ☐ comes after △, ○ comes after ☐, and △ comes after ○.

9.
A change in the lines in the circle; ⦙ comes after ⊜, and ⦸ comes after ⦙.

10. △ △
A change in the dot in the triangle; △ comes after △, and △ comes after △.

11.
12.
13.
14.
15.
16.
17. **Carmen**
18. **Alyssa**
19. **Maddy**
20. **Alyssa**

Unit 7: Numbers 1–20

1. **15**   10 and 5 make 15.
2. **13**   10 and 3 make 13.
3. **18**   10 and 8 make 18.
4. **11**   10 and 1 make 11.
5. **seventeen**   10 and 7 make 17.
6. **fourteen**   10 and 4 make 14.
7. **thirteen**   10 and 3 make 13.
8. **eleven**   10 and 1 make 11.
9. **eleven**
10. **18**
11. **twenty**
12. **12**
13. **fourteen**
14. **twelve**
15. **13**
16. **sixteen**
17. **17**
18. **nineteen**
19. **16**
20. **14**
21. **18**

Singapore Math Level 1A & 1B

22.	**13**	10 + 3 = 13
23.	**17**	10 + 7 = 17
24.	**14**	10 + 4 = 14
25.	**11**	10 + 1 = 11
26.	**20**	10 + 10 = 20
27.	**16**	10 + 6 = 16
28.	**12**	10 + 2 = 12
29.	**19**	10 + 9 = 19
30.	**15**	10 + 5 = 15
31.	**18**	10 + 8 = 18

32.

1 ten **5** ones = **15**

33.

1 ten **10** ones = **20**

34.

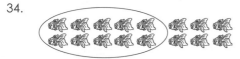

1 ten **6** ones = **16**

35.

1 ten **3** ones = **13**

36. **1** ten and 8 ones = 18
37. **1** ten and 1 one = 11
38. 1 ten and **7** ones = 17
39. 1 ten and **2** ones = 12
40. 1 ten and **5** ones = 15
41. 1 ten and **9** ones = 19
42. Color **14**; 14, 16
43. Color **11**; 11, 20
44. Color **15**; 15, 17
45. Color **19**; 19, 13
46. Color **20**; 20, 15
47. Color **18**; 18, 14

48.
49.
50.

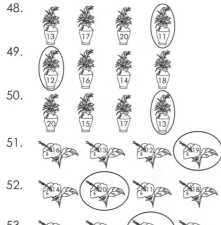

51.
52.
53.

54.	**11, 12**

The pattern increases by 1.

55.	**17, 15**

The pattern decreases by 1.

56.	**14, 12**

The pattern decreases by 1.

57. 1 + 16 = **17**
58. 3 + 11 = **14**
59. 13 − 2 = **11**
60. 19 − 3 = **16**
61. 20 − 4 = **16**
62. **20, 18, 16, 15, 11**
63. **19, 17, 13, 11, 10**
64. **14, 16, 18, 19, 20**
65. **10, 12, 13, 14, 17**

Unit 8: Adding and Subtracting Numbers up to 20

1. **8**, 13
2. **4**, 16
3. **3**, 13
4. **9**, 17

5.

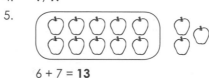

6 + 7 = **13**

6.

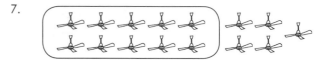

8 + 3 = **11**

7.

8 + 7 = **15**

8.

12 + 8 = **20**

9.	6 + 5 = **11**	6 + 4 = 10
		10 + 1 = 11
	④ ①	

10.	7 + 7 = **14**	7 + 3 = 10
		10 + 4 = 14
	③ ④	

11.	7 + 8 = **15**	7 + 3 = 10
		10 + 5 = 15
	③ ⑤	

12.	9 + 9 = **18**	9 + 1 = 10
		10 + 8 = 18
	① ⑧	

Singapore Math Level 1A & 1B

13. $12 + 5 =$ **17**

(10) (2)

14. $9 + 4 =$ **13**

(1) (3)

15. $11 + 4 =$ **15**

(10) (1)

16. $7 + 8 =$ **15**

(5) (2)

17. $5 + 12 =$ **17**

(2) (10)

18. **15** $- 4 =$ **11**
19. **16** $- 5 =$ **11**
20. $18 -$ **8** $=$ **10**
21. **16** $- 3 =$ **13**

22. $18 - 6 =$ **12**   **8** $-$ **6** $=$ **2**
                        10 $+$ **2** $=$ **12**
(10) (8)

23. $17 - 4 =$ **13**   **7** $-$ **4** $=$ **3**
                        10 $+$ **3** $=$ **13**
(10) (7)

24. $15 - 4 =$ **11**   **5** $-$ **4** $=$ **1**
                        10 $+$ **1** $=$ **11**
(10) (5)

25. $14 - 4 =$ **10**   **4** $-$ **4** $=$ **0**
                        10 $+$ **0** $=$ **10**
(10) (4)

26. $16 - 5 =$ **11**

(10) (6)

27. $12 - 3 =$ **9**

(2) (10)

28. $19 - 8 =$ **11**

(10) (9)

29. $11 - 7 =$ **4**

(1) (10)

30. $15 - 9 =$ **6**

(5) (10)

31. $17 - 9 =$ **8**

(7) (10)

32. $20 - 3 =$ **17**

(10) (10)

33. $6 + 7 =$ **13**

(3) (3)

34. **3** $+ 8 = 11$

35. **13** $- 4 = 9$

36. $12 -$ **5** $= 7$

37. $16 +$ **0** $= 16$

38. $9 +$ **9** $= 18$

39. $15 -$ **6** $= 9$

40. $13 +$ **5** $= 18$

18
(5) (13)

41. **+**
    6, 7, 8, 9, 10, 11, 12, 13

42. **−**
    15, 14, 13, 12, 11, 10, 9, 8, 7

43. **+**
    17, 18, 19

44. **−**
    11, 10, 9, 8, 7, 6

45. **+**
    8, 9, 10, 11, 12, 13, 14, 15, 16, 17

46. **8 + 6 =** $10 + 4 =$ **14**

Eliza has **14** dolls altogether.

47. **18 − 9 = 9**

Imani has **9** stickers now.

235

Singapore Math Level 1A & 1B

48. **6 + 7 = 13**

(3) (3)

Mike colors **13** stars altogether.

49. **4 + 10 = 14**

Sarah bought **14** flowers in 2 days.

50. **15 − 8 = 7**

(5) (10)

Peter has **7** more toy cars than Sam.

Unit 9: Length

1.

2.

3.

4. *Possibe answer:*

Line A ――――――――

5. *Possible answer:*

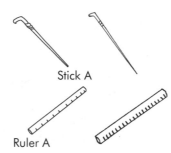

Stick A

Ruler A

6. *Possible answer:*

7. *Possible answer:*

Kite A

8.

9.

10. **tallest**   17. **12**
11. **taller, shorter** 18. **13**
12. **shortest**   19. **14**
13. **highest**   20. **C, 5**
14. **higher**   21. **F, 1**
15. **4**   22. **D, E** or **E, D**
16. **5, 3**   23. | | **A** | |

Review 4

1. **15**   10 and 5 make 15.
2. **16**   10 and 6 make 16.
3. (a) **5**   (e) **D**
    (b) **4**   (f) **C**
    (c) **2**   (g) **C**
    (d) **6**

4. **4 + 7 = 11**   6. **13 − 6 = 7**

(1) (3)   (3) (10)

5. **18 − 7 = 11**   7. **5 + 9 = 14**

(10) (8)   (4) (1)

8. (14)

9.

10. **15, 17**
11. **17, 16**
12. **20, 18, 15, 14, 11**
13. **11, 13, 16, 17, 19**
14. **1** ten **4** ones
15. 10 + 6 = **16**
16. 10 + 10 = 20 = **2** tens **0** ones
17. **16 − 5 = 11**

(10) (6)

Sam has **11** markers.

18. **12 + 8 = 20**

(10) (2)

Natalie pays $**20** for her toy.

19. **18 − 10 = 8**

(8) (10)

He saved $**8** more in February.

20. **13 − 5 = 8**

(3) (10)

Amina has **8** guppies.

Mid-Review

1. **7**
2. **seventeen**
3. **6 + 8 = 14**

(14)
(6) (8)

4. **19 − 6 = 13**

(19)
(6) (13)

5.

6.

7. $20 - 5 = 15$

8. $5 + 7 = 12$

9. $3 + 6 = 9$

10. $16 - 4 = 12$

11. $11 - 11 = 0$

12. **5, 7**
The pattern increases by 1.
13. **square**
14. **triangle**
15. **2nd**
16. **tenth**
17. **20**
18. **1** ten **3** ones
19.

20. (a) **A**   (c) **5**
    (b) **F**   (d) **2** $7 - 5 = 2$
    E: 3 units   (e) **5** $8 - 3 = 5$
    F: 1 unit

21. $13 - 6 = 7$

She has **7** apples left.

22. (a) $11 + 8 = 19$

He saves **$19** altogether.

(b) $11 - 8 = 3$

He saves **$3** more in April than in March.

23. $20 - 7 = 13$

He needs to collect **13** more toy planes.

24. $15 - 9 = 6$

She needs **$6** more.

25. $12 + 4 = 16$

She made **16** bookmarks altogether.

Challenge Questions

1. *Possible answer:*

Check: $3 + 5 + 2 = 10$
$4 + 5 + 1 = 10$

2.

Antwon	Rosa	Kayla
Jonathan	Sean	Cameron

STAGE

3. Mei
Nicholas
Ivana
Simon

Nicholas has the longest ruler.

4.

6 boys went to the movies.

5. *Possible answer:*
$4 + 6 + 7 = 17$ or
$1 + 9 + 7 = 17$ or
$2 + 8 + 7 = 17$

6. The first digit is smaller than 3 so it is either 1 or 2.
The first digit is an odd number so it is 1.
The difference between the first and second digits is 5.
    first digit = 1
    second digit = unknown
    difference = 5

The 2-digit number is **16**.

7. The mouse can travel **5** routes in order to get the cheese.

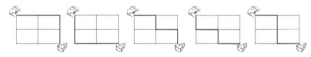

8.

△	○	▭
●	▬	▲
▭	▲	●

9.

Drinking fountain

Mia

Joel

Mia is **3rd** from the drinking fountain.

10. *Possible answer:*

0	3	7
6		2
4	5	1

Numbers **8** and **9** are not used.

11. $1 + 2 = 3$
I am **12**.

12.

12 triangles can be formed from the shape.

Unit 10: Mass

1. **lighter than**
   When the apple on the balance moves upward, this shows it is lighter.
2. **heavier than**
   When the keyboard on the balance moves downward, this shows it is heavier.
3. **as heavy as**
   When the balance is equal, this shows that the apple and mango have the same mass.
4. **3**
5. **5**
6. **6**
7. **10**
8. **4**
9. **7**
10. **3**
11. **5**
12. **dictionary**
    The mass of the book is 5 units, and the mass of the dictionary is 7 units.
13. **box of pencils**
    The mass of the box of pencils is 3 units, and the mass of the file is 4 units.
14. **dictionary**
15. **box of pencils**
16. **box of pencils, notebook, book, dictionary**
17. **7**
18. **5**
19. **4**
20. **2**
21. **kite**
    The mass of the doll is 4 units, and the mass of the kite is 2 units.
22. **teddy bear**
    The mass of the teddy bear is 7 units, and the mass of the toy car is 5 units.
23. **kite**
24. **teddy bear**
25. **doll**
26. **11**
27. **9**
28. **10**
29. **B**
    The mass of Basket C is 10 units, and the mass of Basket B is 9 units.
30. **A**
    The mass of Basket A is 11 units, and the mass of Basket C is 10 units.
31. **A**
32. **B**
33. **A, C, B**

34. **D**
35. **B**
36. **11**
37. **12**
38. **B**
    The mass of Bag C is 8 units, and the mass of Bag B is 7 units.
39. **A**
    The mass of Bag D is 12 units, the mass of Bag A is 11 units, and the mass of Bag C is 8 units.
40. **D, A, C, B**

Unit 11: Picture Graphs

1.

Monkeys	○ ○ ○ ○ ○
Lions	○ ○ ○
Tigers	○ ○
Giraffes	○ ○ ○ ○
Parrots	○ ○

2.

Hopscotch	Soccer	Jumping Rope	Marbles
☆ ☆ ☆ ☆	☆ ☆ ☆ ☆ ☆ ☆ ☆ ☆	☆ ☆ ☆	☆ ☆ ☆ ☆ ☆

3.

Soccer	△ △ △ △ △ △
Kite-Flying	△ △ △ △
Feeding Ducks	△ △
Walking	△ △ △ △ △

4. **4**
5. **5**
6. **turkey burgers**
7. **chicken fingers**
8. 4 − 2 = **2**
9. 5 − 3 = **2**
10. **6**
11. **10**
12. **football**
13. **karate**
14. **swimming, baseball**
15. 7 − 4 = **3**
16. 10 − 4 = **6**

17. 7 + 6 + 10 = 23
    23 + 6 + 4 = **33**
18. **4**
19. **2**
20. **ants**
21. **ladybugs**
22. 7 – 4 = **3**
23. 5 – 2 = **3**
24. 4 + 5 + 7 = 16
    16 + 2 = **18**

Review 5
1. **8**
2. **5**
3. **thermos**
4. **coffee pot**
5. 8 – 5 = **3**
6. 10 – 7 = **3**
7. **5**
8. **2**
9. **6**
10. **9**
11. **D**
12. **B**
13.

	☆		☆
	☆		☆
	☆		☆
☆	☆		☆
☆	☆	☆	☆
☆	☆	☆	☆
☆	☆	☆	☆
Kite-Flying	Riding Bikes	Feeding Birds	Walking
Each ☆ stands for 1 student.			

14. **heavier than**
    When the book on the balance moves downward, this shows it is heavier.
15. **lighter than**
    When the glass on the balance moves upward, this shows it is lighter.
16. **as heavy as**
    When the balance is equal, this shows that the water bottle and telephone have the same mass.
17. **heavier than**
    When the picture frame on the balance moves downward, this shows it is heavier.
18. **8**
19. **12**
20. **3**

Unit 12: Numbers up to 40

1. **26**

2. **13**

3. **30**

4. **31**

5. **21**

6. (a) **twenty**
   (b) **fifteen**
   (c) **thirty-nine**
   (d) **twenty-seven**
   (e) **eleven**
   (f) **forty**
   (g) **thirty-five**
   (h) **twenty-one**
7. (a) **14**
   (b) **24**
   (c) **30**
   (d) **19**
   (e) **26**
   (f) **18**
   (g) **32**
   (h) **13**
8. (a) 30 + 6 = **36**
   (b) 20 + 1 = **21**
   (c) 10 + 7 = **17**
   (d) 20 + 8 = **28**
   (e) 30 + 3 = **33**
   (f) 10 + 4 = **14**
   (g) 20 + 6 = **26**
   (h) 30 + 9 = **39**
9. **3, 5, 35**
10. **2, 1, 21**
11. **3, 9, 39**
12. **4, 0, 40**
13. **1, 6, 16**
14. **2, 3, 23**
15. 2 + 16 = **18**
16. 35 – 5 = **30**
17. 3 + 24 = **27**
18. 1 + 39 = **40**
19. 28 – 9 = **19**
20. (a) **35**
    (b) **17**
    (c) **35**
    (d) **17**
    (e) **17, 22, 35**

21. (a) **16**
    (b) **40**
    (c) 2 + 29 = **31**
    (d) 29 − 2 = **27**
    (e) **27, 31**
22. (a) **40**
    (b) **19**
    (c) 2 + 19 = **21**
    (d) 40 − 5 = **35**
    (e) **21**
23. (a) **14**
    (b) **31**
    (c) 3 + 28 = **31**
    (d) 17 − 3 = **14**
    (e) **25**
24. 2 less than 21
25. 1 more than 37
26. 3 more than 20
27. 2 more than 23
28. 3 less than 18
29. 1 less than 25

     38
     24
     19
     15
     23
     25

30. **11, 17**
    23 − 20 = 3
    14 − 3 = 11
    14 + 3 = 17
31. **24, 29**
    14 − 9 = 5
    19 + 5 = 24
    24 + 5 = 29
32. **30, 40**
    25 + 5 = 30
    35 + 5 = 40
33. **30, 36**
    34 − 32 = 2
    28 + 2 = 30
    34 + 2 = 36
34. **36, 42**
    24 − 18 = 6
    30 + 6 = 36
    36 + 6 = 42
35. **29**
       2 0
     +   9
       2 9
36. **13**
       1 0
     +   3
       1 3
37. **24**
       2 0
     +   4
       2 4
38. **37**
       3 0
     +   7
       3 7
39. **34**
       3 0
     +   4
       3 4

40. (a) **3, 4, 2**
    3, 6
    36
    (b) **1, 6, 4**
    1, 10
    20
    (c) **2, 2, 7**
    2, 9
    29
    (d) **2, 4, 8**
    2, 12
    32
    (e) **2, 7, 7**
    2, 14
    34

41. (a)
Tens	Ones
1	3
+ 1	3
2	**6**

(b)
Tens	Ones
2	4
+ 1	5
3	**9**

(c)
Tens	Ones
3	5
+	2
3	**7**

(d)
Tens	Ones
1	1
+ 2	6
3	**7**

(e)
Tens	Ones
3	0
+	6
3	**6**

42. (a)
Tens	Ones
¹2	9
+	7
3	**6**

(b)
Tens	Ones
¹1	5
+ 1	8
3	**3**

(c)
Tens	Ones
¹2	8
+ 1	2
4	**0**

(d)
Tens	Ones
¹1	9
+ 1	6
3	**5**

(e)
Tens	Ones
¹2	5
+	6
3	**1**

Singapore Math Level 1A & 1B

43.

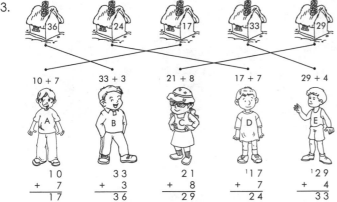

43 answers shown:

36	24	17	33	29

10 + 7   33 + 3   21 + 8   17 + 7   29 + 4

A   B   C   D   E

```
   1 0        3 3        2 1       ¹1 7       ¹2 9
 +   7      +   3      +   8      +   7      +   4
 ─────      ─────      ─────      ─────      ─────
   1 7        3 6        2 9        2 4        3 3
```

44. (a) 27 − 3 = **24**

    (20) (7)

    7 − 3 = 4
    20 + 4 = 24

   (b) 36 − 2 = **34**

    (30) (6)

    6 − 2 = 4
    30 + 4 = 34

   (c) 19 − 3 = **16**

    (10) (9)

    9 − 3 = 6
    10 + 6 = 16

   (d) 25 − 4 = **21**

    (20) (5)

    5 − 4 = 1
    20 + 1 = 21

   (e) 38 − 9 = **29**

    (28) (10)

    10 − 9 = 1
    28 + 1 = 29

   (f) 30 − 3 = **27**

    (20) (10)

    10 − 3 = 7
    20 + 7 = 27

45. (a) **2, 6, 2**
      2, 4
      24

   (b) **3, 7, 3**
      3, 4
      34

   (c) **1, 6, 1**
      1, 5
      15

   (d) **2, 4, 4**
      2, 0
      20

   (e) **3, 3, 4**
      2, 13, 4
      2, 9
      29

46. (a)

Tens	Ones
2	8
−	7
2	**1**

   (b)

Tens	Ones
3	5
− 1	2
2	**3**

(c)

Tens	Ones
1	9
−	6
1	**3**

(d)

Tens	Ones
2	5
− 1	1
1	**4**

(e)

Tens	Ones
3	7
− 1	3
2	**4**

47. (a)

Tens	Ones
²3̷	¹²2̷
− 1	8
1	**4**

   (b)

Tens	Ones
³4̷	¹⁰0̷
− 1	5
2	**5**

   (c)

Tens	Ones
¹2̷	¹⁶6̷
− 1	7
	9

   (d)

Tens	Ones
¹2̷	¹³3̷
− 1	4
	9

   (e)

Tens	Ones
²3̷	¹⁰0̷
−	9
2	**1**

48.

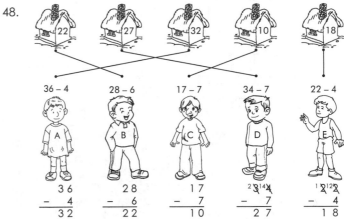

22	27	32	10	18

36 − 4   28 − 6   17 − 7   34 − 7   22 − 4

A   B   C   D   E

```
   3 6        2 8        1 7       ²3̷⁴4̷      ¹²2̷¹²2̷
 −   4      −   6      −   7      −   7      −   4
 ─────      ─────      ─────      ─────      ─────
   3 2        2 2        1 0        2 7        1 8
```

49. 3 + 5 + 7 = **15**

    (2) (3) |
       (10)

    7 + 3 = 10
    3 + 2 = 5
    10 + 5 = 15

Singapore Math Level 1A & 1B

50. $4 + 9 + 6 = \textbf{19}$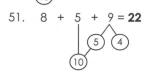

$4 + 6 = 10$
$3 + 6 = 9$
$10 + 9 = 19$

51. $8 + 5 + 9 = \textbf{22}$

$5 + 5 = 10$
$8 + 4 = 12$
$10 + 12 = 22$

52. $7 + 6 + 7 = \textbf{20}$

$7 + 3 = 10$
$3 + 7 = 10$
$10 + 10 = 20$

53. $8 + 6 + 3 = \textbf{17}$

$8 + 2 = 10$
$4 + 3 = 7$
$10 + 7 = 17$

54. $9 + 4 + 5 = \textbf{18}$

$9 + 1 = 10$
$3 + 5 = 8$
$10 + 8 = 18$

55. $8 + 7 + 6 = \textbf{21}$

$8 + 2 = 10$
$5 + 6 = 11$
$10 + 11 = 21$

56. $9 + 6 + 8 = \textbf{23}$

$9 + 1 = 10$
$5 + 8 = 13$
$10 + 13 = 23$

57.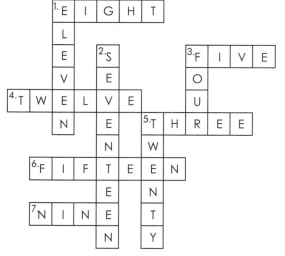

Across
1. $13 - 5 = 8$
3. $8 - 3 = 5$
4. $6 + 6 = 12$
5. $12 - 9 = 3$
6. $10 + 5 = 15$
7. $18 - 9 = 9$

Down
1. $7 + 4 = 11$
2. $20 - 3 = 17$
3. $17 - 13 = 4$
5. $11 + 9 = 20$

58.

$21 + 9 = 30$
He has **30** bookmarks now.

	Tens	Ones
	^{1}2	1
+		9
	3	0

59.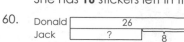

$35 - 19 = 16$
She has **16** stickers left in the end.

	Tens	Ones
	^{2}3	^{15}5
−	1	9
	1	6

60.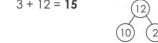

$26 - 8 = 18$
Uncle Jack has **18** eggs.

	Tens	Ones
	^{1}2	^{16}6
−		8
	1	8

61.

$16 + 14 = 30$
Parker has **30** pencils.

	Tens	Ones
	^{1}1	6
+	1	4
	3	0

Unit 13: Mental Calculations

1. $3 + 12 = \textbf{15}$

$2 + 3 = 5$
$10 + 5 = 15$

2. $2 + 17 = \textbf{19}$

$7 + 2 = 9$
$10 + 9 = 19$

3. $11 + 5 = \textbf{16}$

$1 + 5 = 6$
$10 + 6 = 16$

4. $25 + 4 = \textbf{29}$

$5 + 4 = 9$
$20 + 9 = 29$

5. $17 + 10 = \textbf{27}$

$10 + 10 = 20$
$20 + 7 = 27$

6. $22 + 7 = \textbf{29}$

$2 + 7 = 9$
$20 + 9 = 29$

7. $32 + 6 = \textbf{38}$

$2 + 6 = 8$
$30 + 8 = 38$

8. $29 + 10 = \textbf{39}$

$20 + 10 = 30$
$30 + 9 = 39$

9. $8 + 30 = \textbf{38}$

10. $14 + 3 = \textbf{17}$

$4 + 3 = 7$
$10 + 7 = 17$

11. $6 + 20 = \textbf{26}$

12. $15 + 3 = \textbf{18}$

$5 + 3 = 8$
$10 + 8 = 18$

13. $21 + 6 = \textbf{27}$

$1 + 6 = 7$
$20 + 7 = 27$

14. $33 + 4 = \textbf{37}$

$3 + 4 = 7$
$30 + 7 = 37$

15. $10 + 9 = \textbf{19}$

16. $27 + 2 = \textbf{29}$

$7 + 2 = 9$
$20 + 9 = 29$

17. $16 + 10 =$ **26**

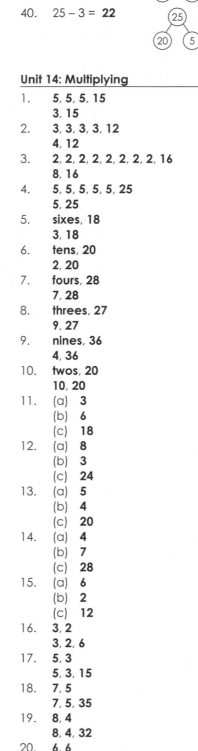

10 + 10 = 20
20 + 6 = 26

18. $7 + 11 =$ **18**

1 + 7 = 8
10 + 8 = 18

19. $13 + 6 =$ **19**

3 + 6 = 9
10 + 9 = 19

20. $20 + 2 =$ **22**

21. $18 - 3 =$ **15**

8 − 3 = 5
10 + 5 = 15

22. $28 - 6 =$ **22**

8 − 6 = 2
20 + 2 = 22

23. $15 - 5 =$ **10**

5 − 5 = 0
10 + 0 = 10

24. $36 - 4 =$ **32**

6 − 4 = 2
30 + 2 = 32

25. $14 - 10 =$ **4**

10 − 10 = 0
0 + 4 = 4

26. $33 - 2 =$ **31**

3 − 2 = 1
30 + 1 = 31

27. $16 - 3 =$ **13**

6 − 3 = 3
10 + 3 = 13

28. $19 - 5 =$ **14**

9 − 5 = 4
10 + 4 = 14

29. $24 - 4 =$ **20**

4 − 4 = 0
20 + 0 = 20

30. $33 - 30 =$ **3**

30 − 30 = 0
0 + 3 = 3

31. $39 - 20 =$ **19**

30 − 20 = 10
10 + 9 = 19

32. $29 - 4 =$ **25**

9 − 4 = 5
20 + 5 = 25

33. $17 - 2 =$ **15**

7 − 2 = 5
10 + 5 = 15

34. $39 - 3 =$ **36**

9 − 3 = 6
30 + 6 = 36

35. $23 - 2 =$ **21**

3 − 2 = 1
20 + 1 = 21

36. $14 - 3 =$ **11**

4 − 3 = 1
10 + 1 = 11

37. $28 - 10 =$ **18**

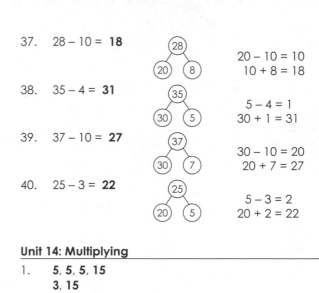

20 − 10 = 10
10 + 8 = 18

38. $35 - 4 =$ **31**

5 − 4 = 1
30 + 1 = 31

39. $37 - 10 =$ **27**

30 − 10 = 20
20 + 7 = 27

40. $25 - 3 =$ **22**

5 − 3 = 2
20 + 2 = 22

Unit 14: Multiplying

1. **5, 5, 5, 15**
   3, 15
2. **3, 3, 3, 3, 12**
   4, 12
3. **2, 2, 2, 2, 2, 2, 2, 2, 16**
   8, 16
4. **5, 5, 5, 5, 5, 25**
   5, 25
5. **sixes, 18**
   3, 18
6. **tens, 20**
   2, 20
7. **fours, 28**
   7, 28
8. **threes, 27**
   9, 27
9. **nines, 36**
   4, 36
10. **twos, 20**
    10, 20
11. (a) **3**
    (b) **6**
    (c) **18**
12. (a) **8**
    (b) **3**
    (c) **24**
13. (a) **5**
    (b) **4**
    (c) **20**
14. (a) **4**
    (b) **7**
    (c) **28**
15. (a) **6**
    (b) **2**
    (c) **12**
16. **3, 2**
    3, 2, 6
17. **5, 3**
    5, 3, 15
18. **7, 5**
    7, 5, 35
19. **8, 4**
    8, 4, 32
20. **6, 6**
    6, 6, 36

Singapore Math Level 1A & 1B

21. **4, 5, 20, 20**
22. **8, 3, 24, 24**
23. **3, 6, 18, 18**
24. **8, 4, 32, 32**
25. **5, 3, 15, 15**
26. **4, 5, 20, 20**
27. **9, 2, 18, 18**
28. **4, 7, 28, 28**
29. **3, 4, 12, 12**
30. **2, 8, 16, 16**

Review 6

1. (a) **12**
   (b) **28**
   (c) **35**
   (d) **11**
   (e) **16**
2. (a) **forty**
   (b) **twenty-nine**
   (c) **thirteen**
   (d) **thirty-eight**
   (e) **fifteen**
3. $20 - 5 = $ **15**
4. $1 + 39 = $ **40**
5. $27 - 3 = $ **24**
6. $4 + 15 = $ **19**
7. $17 - 2 = $ **15**
8. **5, 5, 5, 5, 5, 5, 30**
   fives, 30
9. **9, 9, 9, 27**
   nines, 27
10. (a) **16**
    (b) **31**
    (c) $25 + 3 = $ **28**
    (d) $22 - 3 = $ **19**
    (e) **25**
11. (a) **3, 6, 6**
       3, 0
       30
    (b) **2, 7, 9**
       1, 17, 9
       1, 8
       18
    (c) **1, 6, 7**
       0, 16, 7
       0, 9
       9
12. (a) **8, 24**
       $16 - 12 = 4$
       $12 - 4 = 8$
       $20 + 4 = 24$
    (b) **19, 22**
       $28 - 25 = 3$
       $25 - 3 = 22$
       $22 - 3 = 19$

13. (a)

Tens	Ones
1	2
+ 2	4
3	**6**

(b)

Tens	Ones
1	5
+ 1	3
2	**8**

(c)

Tens	Ones
¹2	5
+	6
3	**1**

(d)

Tens	Ones
¹1	9
+ 1	7
3	**6**

14. (a)

Tens	Ones
1	9
−	8
1	**1**

(b)

Tens	Ones
2	7
− 1	4
1	**3**

(c)

Tens	Ones
³4̶	¹⁰0̶
− 1	5
2	**5**

(d)

Tens	Ones
²3̶	¹⁵5̶
− 1	9
1	**6**

15. $31 + 7 = $ **38**

$1 + 7 = 8$
$30 + 8 = 38$

16. $28 - 10 = $ **18**

$20 - 10 = 10$
$10 + 8 = 18$

17. $5 + 8 + 4 = $ **17**

$8 + 2 = 10$
$5 + 2 = 7$
$10 + 7 = 17$

18. $24 - 8 = 16$; **16**
19. $3 \times 7 = 21$; **21**
20. $8 \times 4 = 32$; **32**

¹2̶¹⁴4̶	
−	8
1	**6**

Unit 15: Dividing

1. (a) **20**
   (b) **4**
   (c) **5**
2. (a) **15**
   (b) **3**
   (c) **5**
3. **4**
4. **5**
5. **2**
6. **3**

7. **4**

8. **10**

9. **5**

10. **4**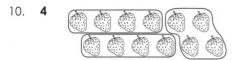

11. **2**

12. **5**
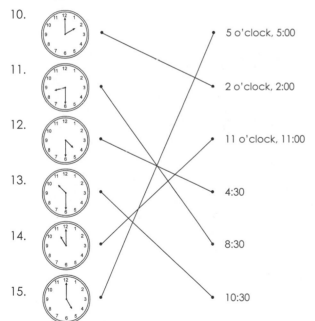

Unit 16: Time

1. **10 o'clock, 10:00**
2. **6:30**
3. **3:30**
4. **8 o'clock, 8:00**
5. **12 o'clock, 12:00**
6. **11:30**
7. **7 o'clock, 7:00**
8. **1:30**
9. **5:30**

10-15. (matching clocks to times)

16. **8 o'clock, 8:00**
17. **7:30**
18. **5 o'clock**
19. **6 o'clock, 6:00**
20. **10:30**
21. **11:30**

Review 7

1. **8 o'clock, 8:00**
2. **9 o'clock, 9:00**
3. **5:30**
4. **2:30**
5. **4:30**
6. **7:30**
7. **3**

8. **5**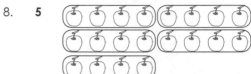

9. **6**

10. **4**

11. **3 o'clock, 3:00**
12. **8:30**
13. **7:30**
14. **12:30**
15. **11 o'clock, 11:00**
16. **5 o'clock, 5:00**
17. **4**

18. **6**

19. **8**

20. **5**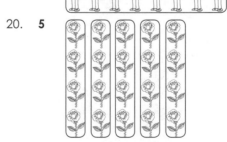

Unit 17: Numbers 1-100

1. (a) **seventy-five**
    (b) **ninety-six**
    (c) **sixty-three**
    (d) **fifty-five**
    (e) **eighty-one**
    (f) **one hundred**

Singapore Math Level 1A & 1B

2. (a) **50**
   (b) **92**
   (c) **64**
   (d) **85**
   (e) **76**
   (f) **99**
3. **4, 5, 45**
  40, 5, 45
4. **6, 3, 63**
  60, 3, 63
5. **5, 7, 57**
  50, 7, 57
6. **7, 9, 79**
  70, 9, 79
7. **9, 0, 90**
  90, 0, 90
8. (a) 5 + 68 = **73**
   (b) 75 − 3 = **72**
   (c) 98 − 4 = **94**
   (d) 8 + 53 = **61**
   (e) 6 + 82 = **88**
   (f) 59 − 7 = **52**
   (g) 56 − 6 = **50**
9. (a) **49**
   (b) **88**
   (c) **74, 88**
   (d) **88**
   (e) **49**
10. (a) **96**
   (b) **64**
   (c) **82**
   (d) **79**
   (e) **96**
11. (a) 80, 84, **88**, **92**, 96, **100**
      84 − 80 = 4
      84 + 4 = 88
      88 + 4 = 92
      96 + 4 = 100
   (b) 66, **69**, 72, 75, **78**, **81**
      75 − 72 = 3
      66 + 3 = 69
      75 + 3 = 78
      78 + 3 = 81
   (c) **74**, **79**, 84, 89, 94
      89 − 84 = 5
      84 − 5 = 79
      79 − 5 = 74
12. (a) 42 + 4 = **46**
     (40) (2)   2 + 4 = 6
                40 + 6 = 46
   (b) 56 + 3 = **59**
     (50) (6)   6 + 3 = 9
                50 + 9 = 59
   (c) 74 + 5 = **79**
     (70) (4)   4 + 5 = 9
                70 + 9 = 79
   (d) 35 + 30 = **65**
     (30) (5)   30 + 30 = 60
                60 + 5 = 65

   (e) 68 + 20 = **88**
     (60) (8)   60 + 20 = 80
                80 + 8 = 88
   (f) 84 + 10 = **94**
     (80) (4)   80 + 10= 90
                90 + 4 = 94
13. (a) **3, 7, 8**
      3, 15
      4, 5
      45
   (b) **4, 5, 5**
      4, 10
      5, 0
      50
   (c) **6, 3, 9**
      6, 12
      7, 2
      72
   (d) **7, 4, 13**
      7, 17
      8, 7
      87
   (e) **8, 6, 14**
      8, 20
      10, 0
      100
   (f) **5, 8, 22**
      5, 30
      8, 0
      80

14. (a)
Tens	Ones
5	3
+ 1	4
6	**7**

   (b)
Tens	Ones
7	0
+ 2	8
9	**8**

   (c)
Tens	Ones
9	1
+	6
9	**7**

   (d)
Tens	Ones
4	4
+ 3	4
7	**8**

   (e)
Tens	Ones
¹2	8
+ 6	4
9	**2**

   (f)
Tens	Ones
¹3	5
+ 4	7
8	**2**

   (g)
Tens	Ones
¹6	8
+ 1	8
8	**6**

246

(h)

	Tens	Ones
	^{1}8	6
+		9
	9	**5**

15.

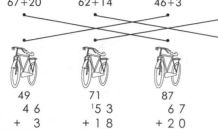

A	B	C	D
67+20	62+14	46+3	53+18

49	71	87	76
4 6	^{1}5 3	6 7	6 2
+ 3	+ 1 8	+ 2 0	+ 1 4
4 9	7 1	8 7	7 6

16. (a) 64 − 3 = **61**

60   4

4 − 3 = 1
60 + 1 = 61

(b) 89 − 6 = **83**

80   9

9 − 6 = 3
80 + 3 = 83

(c) 93 − 4 = **89**

83   10

10 − 4 = 6
83 + 6 = 89

(d) 77 − 5 = **72**

70   7

7 − 5 = 2
70 + 2 = 72

(e) 54 − 6 = **48**

44   10

10 − 6 = 4
44 + 4 = 48

17. (a) **4, 5, 3**
 4, 2
 42

(b) **6, 8, 7**
 6, 1
 61

(c) **7, 6, 6**
 7, 0
 70

(d) **9, 5, 2**
 7, 5
 75

(e) **8, 4, 3**
 5, 4
 54

(f) **9, 3, 1, 2**
 8, 1
 81

(g) **5, 6, 1, 7**
 4, 16, 1, 7
 3, 9
 39

18. (a)

	Tens	Ones
	9	7
−	3	6
	6	**1**

(b)

	Tens	Ones
	7	8
−	1	2
	6	**6**

(c)

	Tens	Ones
	4	6
−	2	5
	2	**1**

(d)

	Tens	Ones
	8	9
−	5	4
	3	**5**

(e)

	Tens	Ones
	^{5}8	^{10}0
−	3	7
	2	**3**

(f)

	Tens	Ones
	^{4}5	^{15}5
−	2	8
	2	**7**

(g)

	Tens	Ones
	^{8}9	^{12}2
−	4	6
	4	**6**

(h)

	Tens	Ones
	^{6}7	^{11}1
−	1	7
	5	**4**

19.

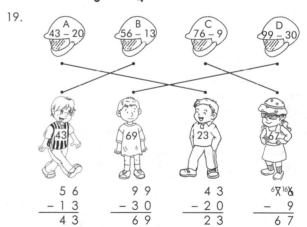

A	B	C	D
43 − 20	56 − 13	76 − 9	99 − 30

5 6	9 9	4 3	^{6}7 ^{16}6
− 1 3	− 3 0	− 2 0	− 9
4 3	6 9	2 3	6 7

20. **80 − 10 = 70**, **70**
21. **65 − 8 = 57**, **57**
22. **72 + 18 = 90**, **90**
23. (a) **18 − 10 = 8**, **8**
 (b) **8 + 3 = 11**, **11**
 (c) **Akira**

Unit 18: Money (Part 1)

1.   **5**
2.   **2**
3.   **5**
4.   **2**

Singapore Math Level 1A & 1B

5. **2**
6. **5**
7. **4**
8. **4**
9. **10**
10. **20**
11. **$16**
12. **$30**
13. **$67**
14. **$58**
15. **$29**
16. **90¢**
17. **95¢**
18. **65¢**
19. **100¢ or $1.00**
20. **45¢**
21.
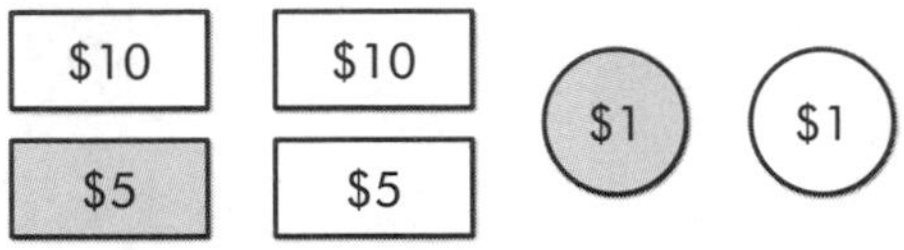
$10
$10
$1
$1
$5
$5

22.
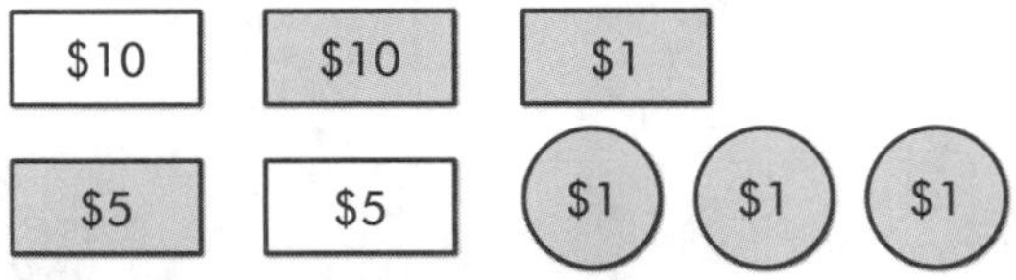
$10
$10
$1
$5
$5
$1
$1
$1

23.
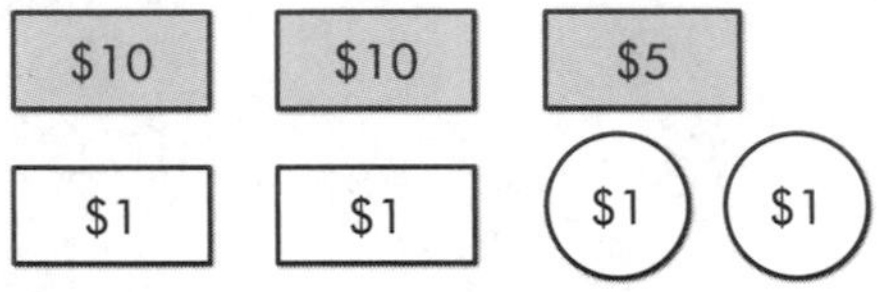
$10
$10
$5
$1
$1
$1
$1

24.
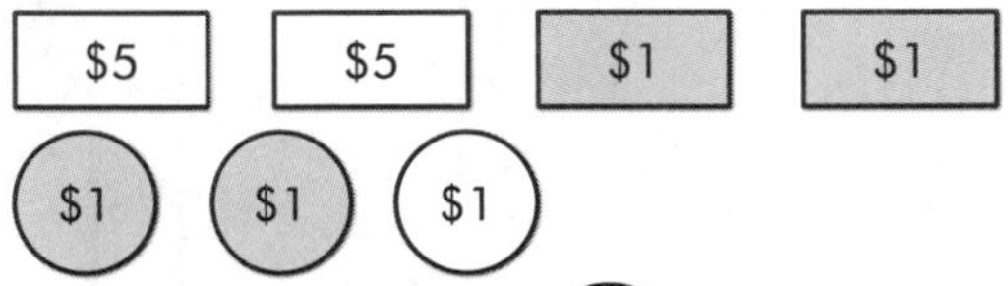
$5
$5
$1
$1
$1
$1
$1

25.
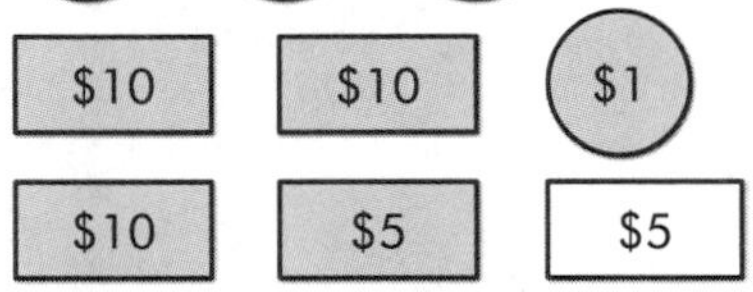
$10
$10
$1
$10
$5
$5

For questions 26–30, accept other possible answers.

26.
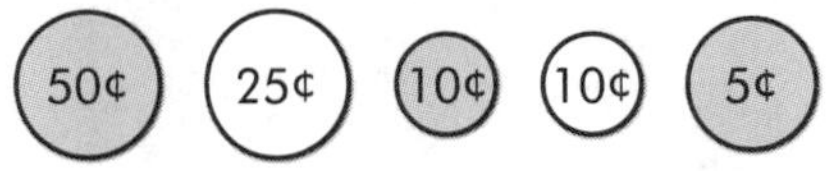
50¢
25¢
10¢
10¢
5¢

27.
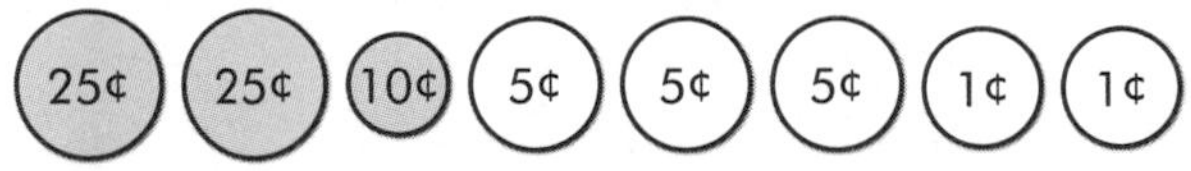
25¢
25¢
10¢
5¢
5¢
5¢
1¢
1¢

28.

25¢
25¢
10¢
10¢
5¢
5¢

29.
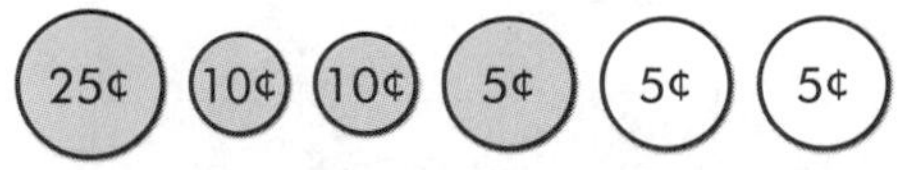
25¢
10¢
10¢
5¢
5¢
5¢

30.
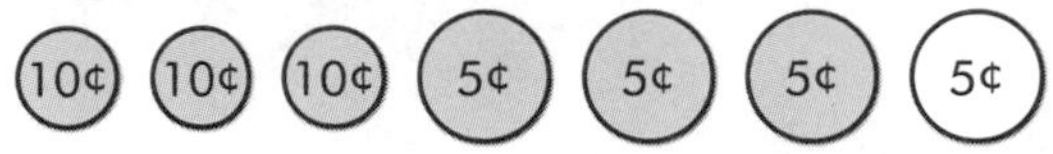
10¢
10¢
10¢
5¢
5¢
5¢
5¢

Unit 19: Money (Part 2)

1. **60¢**

$$\begin{array}{r} 20\ \text{¢} \\ +\ 40\ \text{¢} \\ \hline 60\ \text{¢} \end{array}$$

2. **95¢**

$$\begin{array}{r} 55\ \text{¢} \\ +\ 40\ \text{¢} \\ \hline 95\ \text{¢} \end{array}$$

3. **35¢**

$$\begin{array}{r} {}^{4}\not{5}\,{}^{10}\not{0}\ \text{¢} \\ -\ 15\ \text{¢} \\ \hline 35\ \text{¢} \end{array}$$

4. **110¢**

$$\begin{array}{r} {}^{1}75\ \text{¢} \\ +\ 35\ \text{¢} \\ \hline 110\ \text{¢} \end{array}$$

5. **ruler** and **clip**
65¢ + 15¢ = 80¢

6. **$22**

$$\begin{array}{r} \$\,{}^{1}14 \\ +\ \$\ \ 8 \\ \hline \$\,22 \end{array}$$

7. **$24**

$$\begin{array}{r} \$\,44 \\ -\ \$\,20 \\ \hline \$\,24 \end{array}$$

8. **$77**

$$\begin{array}{r} \$\,17 \\ +\ \$\,60 \\ \hline \$\,77 \end{array}$$

9. **$36**

$$\begin{array}{r} \$\,{}^{4}\not{5}\,{}^{10}\not{0} \\ -\ \$\,14 \\ \hline \$\,36 \end{array}$$

10. **pack of playing cards** and **toy plane**
$8 + $17 = $25

11. **$30**

$$\begin{array}{r} \$\,{}^{1}25 \\ +\ \$\ \ 5 \\ \hline \$\,30 \end{array}$$

12. **$8**

$$\begin{array}{r} \$\,38 \\ -\ \$\,30 \\ \hline \$\ \ 8 \end{array}$$

13. **$20**

$$\begin{array}{r} \$\,{}^{1}12 \\ +\ \$\ \ 8 \\ \hline \$\,20 \end{array}$$

14. **$25**

$$\begin{array}{r} \$\,45 \\ -\ \$\,20 \\ \hline \$\,25 \end{array}$$

15. **skirt** and **blouse**
$38 + $27 = $65

16. **$30**

$$\begin{array}{r} \$\,{}^{1}25 \\ +\ \$\ \ 5 \\ \hline \$\,30 \end{array}$$

17. **float** and **mat**
$16 + $13 = $29

18. **$32**

$$\begin{array}{r} \$\,20 \\ +\ \$\,12 \\ \hline \$\,32 \end{array}$$

19. **$3**

$$\begin{array}{r} \$\,13 \\ -\ \$\,10 \\ \hline \$\ \ 3 \end{array}$$

20. **$13**

$$\begin{array}{r} \$\,25 \\ -\ \$\,12 \\ \hline \$\,13 \end{array}$$

21. $28 + $15 = $43
She has **$43** now.

$$\begin{array}{r} \$\,{}^{1}28 \\ +\ \$\,15 \\ \hline \$\,43 \end{array}$$

22. $90 – $32 = $58

    She has **$58** left.

    $$\begin{array}{r} \$\,{}^8\rlap{/}9\,{}^{10}\rlap{/}0 \\ -\ \ \$\ 3\ 2 \\ \hline \$\ \ 5\ 8 \end{array}$$

23. 60¢ + 25¢ = 85¢

    He spends **85¢** in all.

    $$\begin{array}{r} 6\ 0\ ¢ \\ +\ \ 2\ 5\ ¢ \\ \hline 8\ 5\ ¢ \end{array}$$

24. 90¢ – 55¢ = 35¢

    He saves **35¢** every day.

    $$\begin{array}{r} {}^8\rlap{/}9\,{}^{10}\rlap{/}0\ ¢ \\ -\ \ 5\ 5\ ¢ \\ \hline 3\ 5\ ¢ \end{array}$$

25. $34 + $55 = $89

    She spends **$89** altogether in a week.

    $$\begin{array}{r} \$\ 3\ 4 \\ +\ \ \$\ 5\ 5 \\ \hline \$\ 8\ 9 \end{array}$$

Review 8

1. (a) **36**
    (b) **79**
    (c) 3 + 56 = **59**
    (d) 59 – 3 = **56**
    (e) **64**

2. 4 twenty-five-cent coins •   • $25
3. 3 ten-cent coins •   • $1
4. 2 ten-dollar bills •   • 30¢
5. 5 five-dollar bills •   • $20
6. 6 ten-dollar bills •   • $60

7. (a)
    $$\begin{array}{r} 8\ 3 \\ +\ \ 1\ 5 \\ \hline 9\ 8 \end{array}$$

    (b)
    $$\begin{array}{r} 4\ 6 \\ +\ \ 1\ 2 \\ \hline 5\ 8 \end{array}$$

    (c)
    $$\begin{array}{r} {}^1 3\ 8 \\ +\ \ 3\ 6 \\ \hline 7\ 4 \end{array}$$

    (d)
    $$\begin{array}{r} {}^1 7\ 7 \\ +\ \ 2\ 3 \\ \hline 1\ 0\ 0 \end{array}$$

8. (a)
    $$\begin{array}{r} 9\ 5 \\ -\ \ 4\ 3 \\ \hline 5\ 2 \end{array}$$

    (b)
    $$\begin{array}{r} 6\ 8 \\ -\ \ 2\ 6 \\ \hline 4\ 2 \end{array}$$

    (c)
    $$\begin{array}{r} {}^4\rlap{/}5\,{}^{10}\rlap{/}0 \\ -\ \ 2\ 8 \\ \hline 2\ 2 \end{array}$$

    (d)
    $$\begin{array}{r} {}^7\rlap{/}8\,{}^{13}\rlap{/}3 \\ -\ \ 4\ 7 \\ \hline 3\ 6 \end{array}$$

9.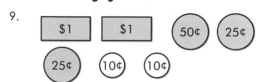

10.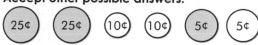

11.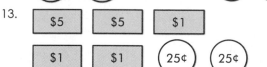

12. **Accept other possible answers.**

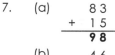

13.
$5	$5	$1
$1	$1	25¢ 25¢

14. 61, **68, 75**, 82, 89
    89 – 82 = 7
    61 + 7 = 68
    68 + 7 = 75

15. 15 + 30 = 45, **45**

16. (a) **25 + 15 = 40, 40**
    (b) **40 – 9 = 31, 31**

17. **30 – 10 = 20, 20**

18. **6 + 5 + 9 = 20, 20**

19. (a) **28 + 18 = 46, 46**
    (b) **50 – 46 = 4, 4**

20. **2**
    $10
    / \
    $5 $5

Final Review

1. 7 – 4 = **3**

2. **5**
   50¢
   10¢ 10¢ 10¢ 10¢ 10¢

3. **5**

4. **lighter than**

5. **7:30**

6. **2, 3, 6**

7. (a) **13 – 3 = 10**
   (b) **27 + 4 = 31**

8. (a) **February**
   (b) **January**
   (c) 9 – 8 = **1**
   (d) 6 – 4 = **2**
   (e) 4 + 9 + 8 + 6 = **27**

9. 88 – 10 = **78**

10. 74 – 34 = **40**

11. **22**

12. **30**
    $$\begin{array}{r} 9\ 0\ ¢ \\ -\ \ 6\ 0\ ¢ \\ \hline 3\ 0\ ¢ \end{array}$$

13. **5**

14. **1 o'clock, 1:00**

15. **12, 21, 36, 47, 63, 79**
16. (a) **36**
    (b) **73**
17. 8 – 3 = **5**
18.

Triangle	☆ ☆ ☆ ☆ ☆
Square	☆ ☆ ☆ ☆ ☆ ☆ ☆ ☆
Circle	☆ ☆ ☆ ☆ ☆ ☆ ☆ ☆ ☆
Oval	☆ ☆ ☆

19. **7, 8, 78**
20. **75 – 45 = 30, 30**
21. **5 × 2 = 10, 10**
22. **4 + 18 = 22, 22**
23. **5**

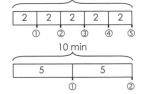

24. **62 – 22 = 40, 40**
25. **50 – 38 = 12, 12**

Challenge Questions

1. The five ways are:
   - **1 kg, 2 kg, 2 kg, 5 kg**
   - **1 kg, 1 kg, 1 kg, 2 kg, 5 kg**
   - **2 kg, 2 kg, 2 kg, 2 kg, 2 kg**
   - **5 kg, 5 kg**
   - **1 kg, 1 kg, 1 kg, 1 kg, 1 kg, 1 kg, 1 kg, 1 kg, 1 kg, 1 kg**

2.
| 1st digit | ? | 3 |
| 2nd digit | ? | |

9 – 3 = 6
3 + 3 = 6
The second digit is 3.
3 + 3 = 6
The first digit is 6.
The number is **63**.

3. A bird has 2 legs. A cat has 4 legs.

Birds	Cats	Total
1 × 2 = 2	2 × 4 = 8	2 + 8 = 10
2 × 2 = 4	3 × 4 = 12	4 + 12 = 16
3 × 2 = 6	4 × 4 = 16	6 + 16 = 22

He has **3** birds and **4** cats.

4. Clock A

   10 min
   | 2 | 2 | 2 | 2 | 2 |
   ① ② ③ ④ ⑤

   Clock B

   10 min
   | 5 | 5 |
   ① ②

   5 + 2 = 7
   The two clocks will chime **7** times in 10 minutes.

5.
$1	$5	$10	$20	Total
✓				$31
				$26
				$35

She has **1 five-dollar bill, 1 ten-dollar bill,** and **1 twenty-dollar bill**.

6.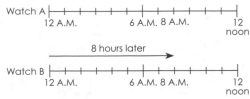

   The actual time is **8 A.M.**

7. 5 + 5 + 5 + 5 = 20
   Therefore, the value of △ is **5**.
   ♡ + ♡ + ♡ + 5 + 5 = 16
   ♡ + ♡ + ♡ + 10 = 16
   ♡ + ♡ + ♡ = 16 – 10
           = 6
   2 + 2 + 2 = 6
   Therefore, the value of ♡ is **2**.

8.
Left page	Right page	Sum
28	29	57
30	31	61

Kenji was looking at **pages 30** and **31**.

9.
1st digit	2nd digit	Difference
2	7	5
2	9	7

I am **29**.

10.

    The cartoon started at **3 P.M.**

11.
1st coin	2nd coin	Sum
50	50	$1
25	50	75¢
10	50	60¢

The greatest amount of money that Elian could receive from his mother was **75¢**.

Singapore Math Level 1A & 1B

Notes

Notes

Notes

Notes

Notes

Singapore Math Level 1A & 1B

Notes